Self-Discipline On Autopilot:

Do The Right Thing, Easily and Habitually

By Peter Hollins

Author and Researcher at
petehollins.com

Table of Contents

Chapter 1: Self-Discipline and the Brain

It's lunchtime and you're faced with a choice:

- a nice healthy salad, or
- a diet-destroying cheeseburger and fries

You've probably encountered dozens of such choices today alone, right? And you made your decisions, for better or worse.

But what exactly allowed you to act with self-control?

Or, if you didn't, why was it so easy to succumb to temptation?

In the chapters that follow, we'll be looking closely at what self-discipline is, why it's so important to a successful life, and how we can cultivate it day by day.

We'll be looking at dozens of different *approaches, techniques, philosophies, and perspectives* to help us become self-determined, resilient, and autonomous individuals.

But throughout, there are really only two main themes we'll be exploring:

1. **Self-awareness**
2. Conscious **action**

Being mindful and awake to what is unfolding in our hearts and minds is half the battle. The other half? Deliberately deciding to **do** something about it. That's why throughout this book, you'll be asked to pause periodically and either:

1. Look within and ask questions to guide **self-awareness**
2. Take **action** right here, right now

Though the material we'll cover is evidence based and makes good sense, the truth is it means nothing if it's not weighed against your own genuine experience and brought to life in action.

Look out for prompts to

➜ **BE AWARE** and
➜ **TAKE ACTION**

They'll allow you to reflect on the material in your own life (awareness), as well as put the ideas to good use (action) by changing your behavior—even if that's only in small ways.

The good news is that no matter where you're starting from today, it is possible to develop better self-discipline, to master your emotions, and to gain a stronger and more resilient sense of purpose. Let's dive in!

The Biology of Self-Control

Let's start with the body.

Though it's tempting to think in abstract terms only, researchers are uncovering evidence that

- willpower,
- control, and
- self-discipline

all have the same biological basis in the brain.

If we can understand the brain regions responsible for self-control and decision-making, then perhaps we can work *with* our brain to make better decisions.

In 2017, scientists (Gross et al.) at the European Molecular Biology Laboratory conducted experiments that revealed a link between two important parts of the brain: the brainstem and the prefrontal cortex.

The researchers believe that these two brain regions are involved in regulating instinctual behavior as well as self-control—a little like the proverbial angel on one shoulder and the devil on the other.

But these "angels" are actually in dialogue:

The prefrontal cortex *acts like a brake* on the impulsiveness of the brainstem.

The experiment began with observing mice who were bullied—yes, really.

Here's how one study went:

- So-called "social defeat" in mice—i.e., being bullied by other mice—resulted in a weakening of the neural connections between the prefrontal cortex and the brainstem in the brains of the mice.
- Those mice with *weaker connections* then behaved more defensively.
- The scientists could also induce the same fear-based response in the mice through the use of certain drugs instead of social defeat.
- In these mice, too, the *connection* between the brain parts was disrupted.

Now, you may be wondering what scared mice have to do with what you choose for lunch.

It's about that dialogue between the two parts of your brain.

It's about the relationship between them.

The connection between the prefrontal cortex and the brainstem is what allows us to *regulate* an instinctual response, i.e., to fight against our instincts.

So, for example, when you're standing on a high diving board with all your friends cheering you on from beneath, you may experience genuine fear, but you push against this and take the leap anyway.

How?

- Your more rational prefrontal cortex is helping to override the survival-based fear coming from your brainstem.

Without that *connection*, the fear signals coming from your brainstem may convince you to climb down off the diving board. Likewise, the impulse to eat the cheeseburger and fries may be dampened by the more rational prefrontal cortex that may tell you, "That's bad for you... ... ... and besides, you ate an hour ago."

Interestingly, scientists noted that in situations that are

- difficult
- tempting, or
- fear-provoking,

the amygdala is still active.

The amygdala is the part of the brain that is responsible for our emotional responses.

What does this mean?

It means that even if we *can* overrule impulsive behavior, we still experience feeling nervous, afraid, or tempted. This is neurological evidence for the saying, *"Courage is not the lack of fear, but feeling the fear and doing it anyway."*

The researchers' conclusions contain two parts:

1. Our inbuilt instinctual urges and impulses are influential
2. Human beings can find ways to **control**, **moderate**, and **regulate** those impulses.

Furthermore, this balance of control is something we can actually observe playing out in the brain—i.e., it's not merely a question of abstract willpower.

Consider another experiment that tells us something interesting about the biology of self-control:

Neuroscientists at the California Institute of Technology gathered thirty-seven people who said they'd had a hard time sticking to diets and maintaining a healthy weight.

- For the experiment, they were asked to fast for three hours.
  - After three hours, the scientists took an fMRI reading of each participants' brain to observe their brain activity.
- The participants were then shown fifty pictures of food and asked to rate each picture on a five-point tastiness scale (in this case, assume that "tasty" means unhealthy and not exactly something you'd choose if you were on a diet, like the participants claimed to be!).
- Next, the researchers noted which foods were rated around 2.5 on the scale, or neutral.
- They then presented *this* food and each of the other forty-nine options, and the participants were told to choose between them. Half of the participants chose the "tastier" option, and half chose the more neutral option.
- Here's the important bit: fMRI scans revealed that **those who picked the healthier food had elevated activity in, you guessed it, the prefrontal cortex**—the dorsolateral prefrontal cortex, to be exact.

It was as though the scientists *saw* in real time the activity of the part of the brain that chips in to say, "No, you shouldn't eat that... ... ... try something healthier, instead."

The "brake" was being applied.

This was self-regulation in action.

Todd Hare, lead author of the *Science* paper, claimed that,

> "One of the differences between people who are good at using self-control and those who are poor at self-control might be the ability to activate the dorsolateral prefrontal cortex." (p. 646)

We can conclude, then, that **self-control, discipline, and the ability to mitigate our instincts is actually a function of a very specific brain region: the prefrontal cortex**.

This is fascinating news.

But it does pose another question: *How can we strengthen the prefrontal cortex?*

Do we have self-control because our prefrontal cortex is strong, or do we strengthen the prefrontal cortex because we have self-control?

In the chapters that follow, we'll be considering the answers to these questions. But we'll also be looking at the question of self-control and self-discipline from many different angles and lenses:

- Your habits
- Your values and principles
- Your physical health and well-being
- Your thought processes
- Your background and history
- Your personality
- Your culture and family
- Your environment
- Your attitude and beliefs

- Your emotions
- Even your spiritual well-being

Neuroscientists can observe brain activity and make inferences about its function. But just because **self-control has a biological basis**, it doesn't mean that that's *all* there is to it. If you take a deep breath and choose the salad over the cheeseburger, is it "because" of your brain? Or is it because of your learned behaviors, your mindset, or your social environment?

The answer is: it's all these things.

BE AWARE: As you start this book, what are your expectations about the changes you'll need to make?

How do *you* frame the issue of self-discipline?

Where did you get these ideas?

We begin with the brain... ... ... but that's only the beginning. What we learn from the two experiments above is that self-discipline is a 360-degree phenomenon, and that what we experience on the emotional, behavioral, and cognitive levels is simultaneously played out on the physical and neurochemical level.

Understanding Delayed Gratification

Let's move on from cheeseburgers to marshmallows... ... ... specifically the now-famous "marshmallow test."

In the late 1960s, Walter Mischel was interested in the idea of self-control, and had a particular question in mind:

Does the ability to delay gratification influence future success in life?

Here's how this famous study was designed:

- Mischel took preschool children and sat each one in a room at a table in front of a marshmallow.
- A researcher then told the child that they were leaving the room, and that meant the child had two choices: Wait a little while for the researcher to return, without eating the marshmallow, whereupon they'd be given more marshmallows, OR if they absolutely couldn't wait, they could eat the marshmallow, but then they wouldn't receive any more. In this case, they'd ring a bell and the researcher would return.
- The researchers were in another room, recording just how long each child could delay gratification—if at all!
- Fast forward a few years and the researchers discovered this: Those children who could wait the longest before gobbling the marshmallow showed better academic performance by the time they were fifteen years old. In other words, the capacity to delay instant gratification was a reliable predictor of future success.

It wasn't just school success, either.

The children able to delay gratification had lower aggression, more social responsibility, higher confidence, and better overall self-efficacy. According to Mischel, **the cognitive skills that allowed the preschoolers to resist the marshmallow were the same ones that enabled more general self-control and self-regulation in all of life.**

Mischel later expounded on a "hot" and "cool" theory where the emotional and instinctual reaction ("go!") was kept in check by the rational, slower, and more neutral reaction ("know").

Sound familiar? It's not unlike the relationship between the brainstem and the prefrontal cortex!

It doesn't matter if your goal is to lose a few pounds, save money for something important, or quit procrastinating—knowing how to delay gratification and check impulsiveness is a key skill that affects your entire life.

It's especially important when you consider that the world is often set up to create, sustain, and reward addictive and impulsive behavior while downplaying long-term consequences (see, the entire advertising industry).

Delayed gratification = the ability to delay the fulfilment of an impulse for immediate satisfaction in favor of a reward sometime in the future.

The term is often used along with concepts of *self-regulation*, *discipline*, and *self-control.*

According to Baumeister et al.'s theory of self-regulation (2007), there are five areas in which we can delay gratification:

1. **Food** (e.g., having a smaller meal rather than a bigger one today to avoid becoming overweight in many years' time)

2.   **Addiction and physical pleasures** (e.g., choosing not to feel the joy of a particular substance right now so you can enjoy health and freedom in the long run)
3.   **Social interactions** (e.g., foregoing a party so you can work or study, even though it's obviously less fun to do so)
4.   **Money** (e.g., foregoing the pleasure of spending on little things today so that you can afford to retire earlier in the future)
5.   **Achievement** (e.g., turning away from momentary distractions to keep focusing on the long-term goal, even though it's not very exciting or rewarding)

As you can see, inhibitory and self-regulating behavior kind of goes against the grain!

It's the ability to *consciously choose* (there's self-awareness and action again!) to feel less good in the moment so that you can feel better in the future. Grasping pleasure in the moment is often the default mode. The ability to value the future over the present, on the other hand, takes

- maturity,
- discipline, and
- control,

so it can never be the default.

Our species has evolved to seek immediate gratification for a good reason: Tomorrow is not guaranteed, and our survival may hinge on us seizing opportunities for pleasure in the here and now. But left to its own devices, this mechanism can result in impulsive and, ironically, self-destructive behavior.

At the same time, constantly delaying gratification and inhibition is not always the best strategy, either. There may well be times when it is better to accept fifty dollars today instead of five hundred dollars in ten years—especially if, for example, you have reason to believe you won't be around in ten years!

But let's be real. If you are able to *consistently*

- eat well,
- turn away from damaging addictions,
- make smart choices that contribute to your long-term development,
- invest money, and
- avoid distractions

... then it's hard to imagine what goal you couldn't achieve.

So, the battle between the prefrontal cortex and the brainstem is simple:

- Impulse vs. conscious choice.
- Pleasure in the moment vs. reward in the future.
- Being a slave to instinct vs. mastering it for your own ends.

You only need to consider how high the global rates are for mental health issues, obesity, addiction, divorce, and debt to see how rare it is to choose something other than instant gratification!

What Does Impulsivity Look Like in Your Life?

BE AWARE: So, be honest, how impulsive are you?

How would *you* score on the marshmallow test?

Don't be so quick to assume that you have no issues with self-discipline merely because certain tasks are not a problem for you. The lack of self-discipline and ability to delay gratification can show up in many different ways in different people's lives.

Take a look at these examples:

- Vicky doesn't like having to compromise, preferring to simply end friendships if they become too much hard work. Her relationships suffer, too, because she constantly chooses the instant gratification of starting a new, fun relationship rather than sticking through thick and thin with the person she's already with.
  - **Consequence:** No relationship lasts longer than a year, and ultimately she feels lonely and aimless.
- Jaden has a wife and loves her, but unable to temper his addiction to pornography, he finds his lack of impulse control eroding the trust in his marriage. On top of this, his addiction to social media and the instant gratification of the online world means he seldom has the patience or attention span to connect in deeper, more meaningful ways with his wife.
  - **Consequence:** He loses the feeling of genuine closeness with her.
- Laura is a student whose life is slowly being ruined by junk food. More than one hundred pounds overweight, she realizes her health and self-esteem are in tatters, and despite knowing she shouldn't, she fritters away the little disposable income she has on high-fat, high-sugar food that she sometimes doesn't even enjoy.

- o   **Consequence:** Laura's low self-esteem starts to poison everything else. She withdraws socially, gives up on dating, abandons her bigger ambitions, and settles for a mediocre job.
- •   Mike is intelligent, passionate, and talented. He has been trying to write a book for nearly ten years. Somehow, he can never seem to muster enough motivation. He cannot work undisrupted on any one task for more than a minute or two before his mind wanders to something more immediately satisfying. After a day of excuses, procrastination, and distractions, he's achieved absolutely nothing. In the moment, it seemed like the obvious choice to watch YouTube videos and read news articles instead of writing.
- o   **Consequence:** As his 40th birthday rolls around, Mike is hit with the sad realization that all these temporary amusements have amounted to nothing, and that his big dream is still just that—a dream.

As you can see, knowing how to be patient, delay gratification, and moderate impulses is about so, so much more than just turning down a sweet treat here and there!

As we'll explore in later chapters, the phenomenon of **self-control, discipline, or curtailing impulsiveness is really about making brain changes that allow you to completely shift your mindset.** It's arguable that a huge portion of what we call self-help and personal development is really just an attempt to master self-control, only in disguise.

BE AWARE: On a scale of one to ten, how well developed do you think your own self-discipline is?

And if you didn't give yourself a high score, what's standing in the way?

Maybe it's:

- Society, laying traps for you at every turn.
- Knowing that even if you do delay gratification, the rewards are not guaranteed and not always proportional (for example, you might pass on the cake today and *still* be overweight in a year's time...).
- You feel bad (depressed, anxious), and that small moment of instant gratification literally feels like all you have going for you right now.
- Because life feels unfair and unpredictable, and if there is a way to succeed and do well, you worry that the rules are complex and not so straightforward (for example, what if restricting calories is actually making you *gain* weight? Is it even possible for people to lose weight? What's the right thing to do when there is so much conflicting advice out there, anyway? Why delay satisfaction when you're not even sure that it will bring you any reward?).
- You don't know *when* the reward will come, and that feels as good as never. Instant gratification, however, is conveniently right here in front of you...
- The fact that you don't really have faith in your own abilities and deep down don't believe that change is possible for you.

TAKE ACTION: Before reading any further, get a hold of a journal or diary where you can monitor your responses to certain questions and keep track of exercises you complete.

➔ **Important: Keep this journal private!**

Something you might be happy to learn is that Mischel discovered that there were in fact easy ways to get his child study participants to wait just a little longer for the marshmallow. When the children sang songs, for example, thought about something else, or covered their eyes so they couldn't see the marshmallow, they were able to wait longer.

So there is hope!

If we understand how our brains work, we can use *practical* tips and tricks to work around our limitations.

Mischel learned through his research that people tend to have better self-control when they have:

a)   **definite time frames** (i.e., they know how long they have to wait to fulfill an impulse) and
b)   when these timeframes are **realistic**.

If you re-read the above bullet list of all the reasons it's difficult to have self-discipline, and then invert them, what you've done is create a road map leading you out of impulsivity.

Let's try it. We can develop greater self-mastery by:

- **Being responsible.** Actively controlling our exposure to discipline-destroying aspects of our culture.
- **Setting smart goals.** Choosing modest, realistic, and achievable goals that you have reason to believe you can actually reach.
- **Cultivating well-being.** Making sure that you're calm, contented, healthy, and balanced within yourself so that you are never relying on the satisfaction of impulses as your sole source of well-being.

- **Being prepared.** Making smart choices to manage unpredictability in the world and taking rational steps to control what you can.
- **Being proactive.** Setting your own goals so you can decide when and how frequently you experience a reaffirming reward.
- **Being committed.** Building your self-confidence so that you can trust in your own ability to improve and be better, even if it takes time and effort.

As you read on, you will discover a wealth of different ways to achieve all the above.

Why Even Bother With Self-Discipline?

You may wonder why we're dwelling so much on the *benefits* of self-discipline. Do you find yourself anxious to skip ahead in the book and start reading all the clever tips and tricks that will help you achieve your goals as quickly and easily as possible?

Pause and just notice that impulse—it may in fact be a sign of lack of discipline!

After all, this hunger for a quick fix is the same as a desire for immediate gratification. Notice this response in yourself. Notice that you're prioritizing:

- The reward
- The satisfying outcome
- The fulfillment of a fleeting desire

Notice, too, what you might be wishing to skip over:

- The effort

- The learning curve
- The process

In impulsive moments, there is one big thing you're not focusing on: the future.

By dwelling on the benefits of self-discipline, you are refocusing your attention on a different pleasure—the bigger one that unfolds later.

If you're staring at an enticing piece of chocolate cake, you may well convince yourself that nothing in the world could be nicer than having it there and then. But then, fast forward a few weeks when staring at yourself in the mirror, and with the taste of the chocolate cake long gone, you may start to realize that feeling healthy, lean, and happy in your own skin was actually worth a lot more to you.

By focusing on the benefits of delayed gratification and greater self-discipline, you keep your eye on the bigger prize and put momentary pleasures into perspective.

To reiterate:

- The **brainstem** is that primitive part of your brain that says, *"Just do it! Now is all that matters!"*
- But the **prefrontal cortex** is the more evolved part that allows you to pause and say, *"Your actions have consequences. How will your behavior in the present unfold? Is it what you want? Your wants and desires are not always an indication of the best possible action, and things that feel good right now are not necessarily good for you... "*

It's all a question of which voice you choose to listen to. *That* voice will then become stronger over time.

The benefits of allowing your prefrontal cortex to step in and help you act with rational conscious choice include:

<u>Better health</u>

- You won't be a slave to addictive, unhealthy foods, and you won't routinely take in more food than you need, so you spare yourself the health problems that come with excess weight and obesity.
- You also lessen the chances of being addicted to other substances—caffeine, alcohol, nicotine, or recreational drugs—that rob you of your free will and undermine your quality of life.

<u>Better academic or work performance</u>

- A study by Duckworth and Seligman (2005) found that self-discipline correlated with better educational outcomes in children, including better attendance and higher grades. Here, self-discipline was directly related to lower screen time and fewer distractions.
- For adults, Converse, Pathak, and DePaul (2012) found that greater self-control predicted increased pay and better prestige.

<u>Better relationships</u>
- Knowing how to regulate strong emotions, how to set aside your own desires and focus on others during listening, and how to be patient all lead to

better interpersonal connections, whether that's with family, friends, or colleagues.

- Self-discipline means you're able to take responsibility for yourself while drawing good boundaries.
- Things like compassion and perspective-taking can only happen when we are able to voluntarily pause our own desires in the present and focus on other people. Just as short attention spans lead to shallow work, poor self-control in relationships leads to shallow and unsatisfying connections with others.

<u>Greater chance of achieving goals</u>

- Face it: In life, the most impressive and satisfying goals are never those that happen merely by accident. Rather, the things we most want to achieve take sustained effort over a long period of time.
- If we are constantly trapped in the present, distracted by momentary rewards, we never build the momentum for something greater, be that creating something unique, building a business, achieving a fitness or athletic goal, developing a new skill, or enduring the rigors of tertiary education.

<u>Better mental health</u>

- Those with good self-discipline trust themselves and have higher self-esteem and maturity.
- They feel more resilient because they know they are capable of holding their own in the face of distraction or temptation.

- Knowing how to anchor in your own will and self-regulate is a big part of being a mature, well-rounded adult.

<u>Less criminal behavior</u>

- This one goes without saying!

Really, there is just one big benefit that comes from better discipline, and it's this: *the ability to be in control of your own life.*

It's the satisfaction that comes with knowing that **you** are the driving force behind your thoughts, feelings, and actions… and not something external to you.
Many of us think of self-discipline as a boring and difficult thing, almost like a punishment, right? We imagine a kind of internalized drill sergeant whose job in life is to make us unhappy and keep us away from what we really want.

But let's try to reframe this:

Self-discipline and self-control are actually the only means we have to create more freedom for ourselves—freedom to choose what we want our lives to be.

Though it may take practice and some trial and error, being in command of ourselves is actually the happier, more balanced, and calmer state of mind. Deep down, we don't *really* want

the piece of cake,
the quick fix, or
the distracting social media post.

What we really want is **freedom**.
To be in charge of our own lives.

If we constantly remind ourselves of this fact, then we are constantly putting ourselves back in control and inviting our prefrontal cortex to make the final decision.

Self-discipline is not a *punishment*. It's a *privilege*.

TAKE ACTION: In your journal, take a moment to think about the benefits you'd most like in the various areas of your life, such as health, relationships, etc.
In what ways are you most ready to improve?
What part of your life is crying out most for transformation?

<u>**Willpower Fatigue**</u>

Self-discipline is like a muscle—the more you exercise it, the stronger it gets. The stronger it gets, the easier it finds certain tasks, and eventually what was once difficult becomes easy.

BUT self-discipline is also like a muscle in the sense that it can get worn out and depleted.

It needs to rest just like your muscles do. The strongest person in the world can "spend" their muscle strength in a hard training session, and then be utterly weak until they rest up and recuperate. Any strength trainer will tell you that resting your muscles and allowing them to recover is a big part of what makes them stronger in the long run.

People tend to think of willpower as an all-or-nothing thing—we either have it or we don't. But **willpower is best thought of as a tank that can fill and empty throughout the day and can be influenced by our choices and environment**.

A now-famous study published by the National Academy of Sciences showed what happened when psychologists examined 1112 judicial rulings.

In these cases, a judge needed to decide whether a criminal should be released from prison on parole. The researchers were surprised to discover that the judges' choices appeared to be most influenced not by the unique cases in front of them, but by something else: the time of day.

Namely:

- Favorable rulings tended to be made 65% of the time if held in the morning, but chances of being granted parole would drop as the day wore on.
- After lunch, the positive-ruling rate shot back up to 65%. But as the hours rolled by again, this rate again dropped steadily downward, until it was *near 0% at the close of day.*

It doesn't take a genius to guess why. The judges were simply getting tired!

After lunch, somewhat refreshed, the judges were able to give the cases their full and impartial attention. But with each passing hour, their "decision fatigue" increased and they made less charitable judgments. It didn't matter whether the crime was rape or murder or fraud—the pattern was consistent. It was as if the decision-making muscle of each judge was getting worn out and less and less able to function correctly as the day wore on.

So what can we conclude?

1. The judges didn't exactly have high willpower or low willpower—rather, *they depleted what willpower they had.*
2. On a less serious note, always try to schedule your parole hearings for the morning!

In the same way, that time you cheated on your diet last Tuesday doesn't mean you had low willpower—it just meant that your willpower current's account was overdrawn that day... perhaps it had already been spent on something else!

So-called **decision fatigue** can also be understood as **willpower fatigue.**

You can say no to the temptation once (that's one rep of your willpower muscle) and then say no to it again another dozen times later in the day (that's more reps). But come the evening, that poor willpower muscle is worn out.

So you arrive home after a long hard day and think, "Well, I've been so good. I deserve it," and you finally succumb to temptation. This is not unlike what weight trainers call muscle "failure"—you literally cannot use the muscle anymore.

Crucially, your willpower muscle (your prefrontal cortex) is responsible for *a lot* of different jobs throughout the day, and spending all your will on one task means it's not available for another task.

For example, you may have spent all day at work:

- Solving problems
- Making decisions
- Avoiding temptations
- Choosing between options
- Resisting distractions

When you get home and it's time to go to the gym, though, you suddenly feel "too tired" even though you've been sedentary for hours.

You're not lazy—you really *are* tired. But what is exhausted is not your body, but your sense of willpower and self-control.

➜ Think of it as different currencies; you can spend dollars in one moment and euros and yen in the next. But ultimately, it's all money, and you only have so much of it to spend.

BE AWARE: When was the last time your willpower failed?

What time of day was it?
What was the context?
What made it so difficult to maintain discipline at that moment when you had maintained it at other times?
If you can't think of anything, stay alert all throughout today and notice how your sense of self-control waxes and wanes.

How to Protect Your Willpower

So how do you cultivate and improve your own sense of self-discipline?

Well, it's not by magically creating more willpower—that's impossible.
Instead, it's by **protecting and managing the willpower** you do have.

Here are a few simple ways to do that—notice that in each case, you are NOT required to strongarm your way through things and valiantly fight off temptation.

➔ Remember that you can only be strong for so long.
➔ You need a strategy that will still be in place for all those times when your willpower muscle is fatigued and replenishing.

Do the Most Important Thing First

This is only logical: *Prioritize the task that is most important and demands the most of you.* Many people do not really lack willpower at all but have mismanaged their willpower and wasted it on the wrong thing.

A good habit is to **assign yourself just three things to do every day**.

• Choose no more than three tasks that you are unwilling to leave unfinished by the end of the day.

- Ask yourself, "Which thing would, if completed, make me feel most satisfied and accomplished by the end of today?" Then do that thing first.
- You can tackle other less important ones later if you complete the important three, but do not allow these secondary tasks to derail or distract you.

Example: You might be the kind of person who is most energetic and alert at 11 a.m. every morning. You put a fence around your best two or three hours and dedicate this time and energy to your most important goals.

Instead of tiring yourself out on boring low-level work, you spend this time strategizing, creating, solving problems, or tackling the meatier issues.

Give Yourself Fewer Decisions

Plenty of self-help advice out there tells you to "just decide to do it." That's well and good, except you now know that *the ability to decide is not infinite.*

Instead, treat your capacity for decision-making as a limited resource to guard. Reserve it for situations that genuinely need it most.

The other stuff? You can put that on autopilot. **If you can make something automatic, then you no longer have to make a decision about it**—or rather, you make a decision once and move on.

Example: If you keep finding that the chore of deciding what's for dinner every day is depleting your willpower too much, then stop giving yourself that decision.

- Set up a meal order service.
- Get someone else to cook for you.
- Just eat the same thing every day.
- Batch cook everything once a week and label your meals so that you know ahead of time exactly what you're eating, no further thought required.

It can be a waste of your time and energy to mull over improving your decision-making process. Instead, just stop making as many decisions!

This is what schedules and habits are designed for—to take away your choice. You could deplete your willpower trying to decide whether you should do X or Y this evening. But if you have a schedule, you've already solved the problem—just consult the schedule and do that.

Don't Beat Yourself Up

You can get pretty far in life just by:

- simplifying,
- budgeting your willpower and energy, and
- making the right thing the easiest and most automatic thing.

But even *still*, you will occasionally make a choice you later regret. We are all fallible, and perfection is not possible. This means we also need a strategy for dealing with inevitable slip-ups.

The best strategy? To avoid falling into self-admonishment and despair—primarily because this approach will make you less likely to carry on!

Rather, **be compassionate with yourself.**

Recover as quickly as possible by accepting the mistake, then taking immediate action in the right direction again.

Example: You may cheat on your diet and feel awful. But forgive yourself and **make your very next decision a good one**. Even better, allow your remorse to be put to good use and ask yourself *why* you failed and what you can do to be better next time. Self-awareness + conscious action, always.

Remember, you will always be most effective and a far better learner if you take shame and blame out of the equation.

TAKE ACTION: Make a to-do list for today's tasks, focusing on just three most important items, and do them all when you're feeling strongest. Notice how you feel.

Chapter Takeaways:

- To live a more self-disciplined life, we need to understand only two main principles: 1) Be aware and 2) take conscious action.
- Self-discipline has a biological and neurological basis—but though it starts there, that's not where it ends. Our decisions come down to opposing influences from our more primal and instinctual hindbrain and our higher prefrontal cortex. The degree to which we have self-control is the degree of connection between these two parts.

- Delayed gratification is the ability to delay the fulfilment of an impulse for immediate satisfaction in favor of a reward sometime in the future. It's an essential part of a self-disciplined life. By understanding the reasons you tend toward instant gratification, you can remove them.
- By focusing on the benefits of delayed gratification and greater self-discipline, you keep your eye on the bigger prize and put momentary pleasures into perspective. Of all the many benefits, the greatest is the real sense that you are in control of your own life—i.e., more freedom.
- Willpower is like a muscle—it builds with repeated use but can get fatigued, so it needs to be replenished. Protect and manage your willpower by doing the most important tasks first, simplifying life so you have fewer decisions (by automating or delegating), and quickly forgiving slip-ups when they happen.

Chapter 2: The Mental Roadblocks That Prevent Our Progress

So, we know that self-discipline has a biological basis, and that if we can master it, we can derive countless benefits in life. We also know that a big part of self-control is to remember the future, i.e., resist instant gratification. The best way to do that is to realize the limits of our willpower and plan accordingly.

Sounds good, but if it's that simple, why don't more people have better self-discipline?

BE AWARE: Before reading on, pause and really be honest with yourself. If you feel that you currently lack self-discipline, what do you think is standing in your way?

The Status Quo Bias, and Why We Resist Change

In 1988, researchers William Samuelson and Richard Zeckhauser conducted a range of experiments designed to explore a certain kind of cognitive bias. One experiment went like this:

- Participants were told to imagine they'd inherited a lot of money. They were then asked to choose how they would invest it, given a series of fixed options.
  - Some participants were given a "neutral version"
  - Others were given a "status quo bias version."
- In the neutral version, they were only told that they'd inherited the money and needed to choose how to invest it, with all choices being valid.
- In the status quo version, they were told they'd inherited money, but that it was already invested in some way. They were still given options to re-invest it differently if they wanted to.

Consider right now what *you* might do in this second scenario—leave the money where it is already invested (i.e., retain the status quo) or make a deliberate change?

Samuelson and Zeckhauser's results showed that in the second scenario, **people tended to stay with the status quo... regardless of the alternatives they were offered.**

In fact, the more alternative options offered, the more people tended to want to just stick with the situation they were already in. This becomes even more pronounced when you compare it to the neutral group, who chose alternatives according to their perceived merits—and what was presented as the status quo to the second group was no more or less attractive as an option when presented to the first.

The conclusion?

→ **People have a bias towards favoring the status quo, despite its objective benefits and drawbacks.**
→ **Status quo bias = the preference for your situation (any situation, even a bad one!) to remain the same.**

It's a major roadblock in the way of developing better self-discipline. Sometimes, when trying to make significant life changes, you may get frustrated with yourself and wonder, *If I want X so badly, why don't I just do it already?!*

The answer may be, at least in part, that you simply prefer what you know.

This bias partly explains why people…

- choose to remain living in a home that is objectively bad in many ways, rather than moving to one that is better.
- tend to order the same meal at a restaurant over and over again, despite good reason to believe that there are other potentially delicious things to try.
- don't like brands or shop layouts changing.
- are more likely to vote for an incumbent than a challenger—even if the incumbent is demonstrably awful.

Picking the status quo and deciding not to make a change is a strategy not without merit. After all, staying as you are conserves energy (and recall that you only have a limited willpower budget). If something has broadly worked before, why risk changing that and potentially making things worse, right?

Unfortunately, **this bias holds even when the potential benefits of staying put are obviously outweighed by the costs of not changing.**

Unless we are making conscious decisions with open eyes, we risk defaulting to a cognitive bias that doesn't necessarily serve us.

- At best, we miss out on opportunities to grow and be better.
- At worst, we actually "choose" (by failing to choose) the worse option instead of the better one.

Staying in the same situation may in fact be the most rational choice—but if you act from genuine logical and conscious rationality, then you are not under the spell of the status quo bias.

Likewise, making a change just because you can may also be the less rational decision and may represent a cognitive bias of its own.

What matters is **self-control**—that you are deciding consciously and rationally.

The status quo bias is to blame any time we are ignoring choices and irrationally choosing something not because of its inherent benefits, but simply because we want to maintain the status quo.

It may be pointless to get caught up in overly psychological explanations about why you are resistant to change (are you unconsciously jeopardizing yourself? Does it have something to do with your mother?!) since the status quo bias may be enough all on its own to prevent us from taking action.

The status quo bias rears its head when we make all kinds of decisions, whether they're

- small and inconsequential (what cereal shall I have for breakfast?) or
- significant and important (shall I leave my spouse/job/home country and start a whole new life?).

Occasionally, the status quo bias may be especially pronounced in a person whose life seems marked by fearful inertia—think of the person who has stayed in the same life situation *for decades*, never changing since the status quo is... well, good enough.

TAKE ACTION: In your journal, write down an ambitious goal you'd like to achieve. Challenge yourself to choose something that you're a little afraid of. Then, let it sit there for a while.

Notice any resistance or any excuse your mind jumps in with to tell you why this goal is impossible.

One quick way to break out of the status quo bias? Remind yourself of an important truth:

→   **Not choosing is also a choice.**

Even if it feels like staying as you are is a way to abstain from making a choice, in reality, choosing to maintain an active choice is a decision—one that can bring both positive and negative consequences.

When we choose not to change, we may be entertaining a certain attitude toward risk. In an (often unconscious) accounting, we appraise the situation. We estimate:

- our chances of success,
- the cost of making changes,
- the likely drawbacks,
- the possible benefits of doing something different, and
- the risks of the unknown.

Our choice not to change comes down to the accuracy of these estimations.

In the next section, we'll explore a few more related concepts that factor into these assessments.

The Trap of the Sunk Cost Fallacy

The sunk cost effect = the increased tendency for people to continue with an endeavor if they've already spent time, money, or resources on it.

According to Christopher Olivola, who is an assistant professor of marketing at Carnegie Mellon's Tepper School of Business, "That effect becomes a *fallacy* if it's pushing you to do things that are making you unhappy or worse off."

The sunk cost fallacy = another trap on the road to self-discipline because it keeps us tied to what isn't working.

Let's consider an example.

Liam has been seeing Caitlyn for three years now. The first year was good, the second was a bit more difficult, and it seems like the third year was nothing more than constant fighting.

In the second year, Liam and Caitlyn both realized they had radically different ideas about where their relationship was going, but they pushed through. For both, the relationship was the longest they had ever been in, and they were admired in their friendship group as being an ideal couple. So both unconsciously thought, "Well, we've come this far. We'd better keep going... "

In the third year, they had had more fights and make ups than either of them could count. But now, they had both invested even more time into the failing relationship. They had been through so much pain and difficulty together, it almost seemed like a shame to quit. Would it all have been for nothing, all the tears and drama?

So, they carried on.

When Caitlyn fell pregnant and they had a baby, the sunk cost fallacy was well underway. "There's no chance of breaking up now. We have a baby."

But wait, the story doesn't end there.

Fast forward a few years and Liam and Caitlyn are still miserable, but now they're married, with a giant mortgage and two more kids. A businessman (or a gambler) would say they were continuing to "throw good money after bad." They've come so far; there's no point in quitting now, right?

*Sometimes, though, both Liam and Caitlyn look back at the early days, to the second year of their relationship, and realize something: **It would have been easier to call it quits then.***

Sticking it out only made it more difficult to leave, as they invested more and more into a lost cause. By staying as they were, they only got stuck more and more firmly in a trap that became progressively more difficult to escape. Now leaving is a near impossibility.

The fallacy comes down to not realizing this:

➜ **What you've invested in a lost cause is already gone.**

It's a question of faulty appraisals. You may feel that continuing on a path will somehow redeem or recoup what you've already invested, but it won't.

- Option 1: If Liam and Caitlyn had split earlier on, they would have "lost" those two years. But those two years were lost anyway!
- Option 2: By staying together, they turned two bad years into twenty—this is the awful outcome of allowing the sunk cost fallacy to influence decision-making.

The trick that keeps you in the trap is the thought that, "If I keep going, the game is still in play and something could still happen that would make everything I've already invested worth it."

But in truth, it seldom works out this way.

How do we get around this bias?

First, we need to think rationally and remember the undeniable fact:

➜ **What you've invested in a lost cause is already gone.**

Those costs are "sunk."

They're never coming back.

It's over.

You should *not* factor what you have already spent into the current decision you are making. Instead, we should only take into account what is *currently* true for us and the actual options we have in front of us.

Here's another example:

> *You've paid in full for a course, but you quickly realize the content is not what you imagined, and you derive little enjoyment or use out of it. It's pretty disappointing, but what do you do now?*

If you say, "Well, I've paid for it. It would be such a waste if I didn't continue... " then you'll force yourself to keep going despite knowing rationally that the course has little value. In doing so, though, you waste your time!

The truth is, whether you attend the course or not, the money is already spent.

So, no matter what you do, it's gone.

The costs are already sunk.

There is no choice that you can make that will mean the money *isn't* spent, so you can safely remove that factor from your decision-making process.

Instead, consider:

- Are you enjoying the course?
- Is it useful or appropriate or relevant?
- Do you want to keep doing it?

These are the questions to ask when trying to make your decision.

You should **focus on the benefits of current and future possibilities, not on what cannot be changed in the past**.

Consider: If you abandon the course early on, you at least still have your time—time you could use making back the money you wasted or pursuing something else of value.

Human beings are not always rational decision-makers. We are all susceptible to biases and fallacious thinking—and when the stakes are high, even more so! We tend to see things in overarching narratives instead of just looking at the situation in front of us and how we can maximize it for the potential future.

The sunk cost fallacy is strongly connected to another cognitive bias: **"Commitment bias" = the tendency to continue supporting things simply because we've already made a commitment to doing so.**

Of course, sticking to our commitments is an admirable thing. But what about when doing so actually penalizes you?

Consider this example.

> *You've gone out to buy some new paint for your home: a charming shade called Goose Poop Green. You genuinely loved it at first, and so you bought ten*

cans. But after painting one room this color, you're not so sure.

Wanting to avoid the embarrassment of changing your mind, though, you stick to your original choice and keep on painting the walls green, even though you're actively starting to loathe the color...

The truth is, though, that whether the mistake sits in ten cans of hideous green paint, or it sits out there on every wall of your home, it's still a mistake!

It's more rational, in this case, to break your original ten-can commitment (not to mention write off the cost) and stop the problem from becoming any worse by doing something else.

How?

TAKE ACTION: If you're feeling trapped in a situation but afraid of calling it quits, remember this:

- **Focus on future costs and benefits, not past commitments**. Do this by asking, "Can I change what I've already spent/invested/committed to?
  - If not, then discount that piece of information and focus *only* on what you do moving forward.
- **Forgive yourself, let go of guilt, and move on**. It's normal to feel remorseful, guilty, or obligated when you're tangled up in something suboptimal. But rather than focus on *how bad it feels to waste*, keep turning your mind to *action*. Whatever you do, don't make decisions exclusively based on your emotions.
  - When you feel a pang of guilt and wastefulness, tell yourself, "That money/time/effort is already gone."

- **Stop investing.** In 1980, behaviorist Richard Thaler originally explained the sunk cost fallacy as a phenomenon where "paying for the right to use a good or service will increase the rate at which the good will be utilized." If you keep investing in a course of action, you only tie yourself more strongly to that course and make it harder to disentangle later.
  o Rather, **stop and reflect** before going further down the path.

We can all get trapped by this fallacy now and then, whether it's in big ways (sticking out expensive university degrees we know we shouldn't be doing) or small ways (pushing through with a boring book or a movie we're not actually enjoying).

But if we can take regretful emotions out of the picture and keep our attention on what we can control (our actions right now), we give ourselves the best chances of minimizing the consequences of a bad choice we've already made.

This is a powerful form of self-discipline to master.

Working With Gain, Loss, and Regret

To explain the next cognitive bias that gets in the way of real self-control and personal mastery, consider the following scenario.

- Your friend tells you they will flip a coin.
- If it's heads, they'll give you twenty dollars.
- If it's tails, *you* give *them* twenty dollars.

So what do you think—do you want to play this game?

Chances are, the answer is no, and the reason for this is what behavioral psychologists call **loss aversion, which is the cognitive bias that sees losses as more psychologically significant than gains of the same size**—in this case twenty dollars.

In our example, a *potential loss* of twenty dollars somehow feels bigger and more significant than a *potential gain* of the same amount.

Amos Tversky and Daniel Kahneman were the first to explore and expand on the idea of loss aversion and how it impacts how people process value and reward, and how this in turn influences their behavior. This matters since it threatens to undermine what we are trying to cultivate in this book: self-discipline and the ability to rationally and consciously choose the best course of action.

A professor of psychology at Stanford University, Russell A. Poldrack conducted a study on this very behavior and found that when participants were offered the opportunity to gamble with real money, they showed two interesting tendencies:

- Increased activity in reward centers in the brain, in direct proportion with an increase in the potential **reward**.
- But, as the potential **loss** increased, the brain activity also decreased.

Researchers led by Poldrack found evidence for a neurological basis for what Tversky and Kahneman had theorized decades before—**the brain overall showed a stronger reaction to possible losses than to possible gains.**.

What's more, they discovered that individuals could also vary somewhat in their "loss sensitivity," suggesting that those people who we would describe as risk-averse, for example, actually have brains that show greater sensitivity to both losses and gains.

Scientists are still picking apart all the complex ways the brain processes risks and rewards, but to summarize their conclusions so far, we can say that for most people, **the pain of losing is roughly twice as powerful as the pleasure of gaining**.

Imagine your friend now suggests that they toss the coin again, but the rules are different:

- If it's heads, they'll give you forty dollars
- If it's tails you only have to pay them twenty dollars.

Are you more interested in the game now?

Given what the researchers discovered about people's tendency to prefer avoiding loss over acquiring gains, your answer might be yes. It's not just money, though, but *anything* perceived as valuable—for example, time, resources, or energy.

The fact that this bias exists is understandable—our ancient ancestors survived by hyper focusing on potential loss (which might spell death or ruin) while downplaying potential gains (which are great and all but not exactly something you need to prepare for because whether it happens or not doesn't impact your survival).

Marketers, politicians, and salespeople understand this well and activate the fear of loss in their audience more than they do the anticipation of reward. Even a preacher might dwell on the pain of eternal damnation and hellfire instead of pointing out the benefits of a heavenly paradise!

➔ As fascinating as this all is, what can it tell us about becoming more effective, rational human beings with well-developed self-control?

We first need to understand that loss aversion is part of our psychological makeup and be aware of how it is factoring into our decision-making processes. Next, we need to be aware of the fact that **loss aversion may be preventing us from taking the well-calculated risks that will genuinely improve our lives**.

If we always underestimate potential rewards, we may forego making positive changes (not unlike what we do with the status quo bias!). Letting loss aversion dominate not only our financial decisions but also those concerning our personal development and relationships means we are leaving some of our potential unfulfilled.

Self-control, then, is not always about reining in unhealthy or damaging impulses; it's also about making sure that we act in such a way as to:

- Challenge ourselves to explore our full potential
- Face our fears
- Push ourselves outside our comfort zones (now you know why we began the book with self-discipline benefits!)

We need to **be aware** of biases at work within us, **then act** accordingly to offset them where necessary.

You'll know that loss aversion is a problem for you if:

- You feel unable to handle *any* risk at all, even if it's very minor.
- You often look back and wish you had acted more decisively or bravely, especially after maintaining the status quo proved to be more trouble in the long run after all...
- You get overwhelmed with "analysis paralysis" when trying to predict every tiny possible outcome, or control for every bit of chance or randomness.
- You avoid new challenges and tasks for fear of looking stupid, making a mistake, or somehow jeopardizing your current position.
- You often look at others and envy the changes they make for themselves, but think that you could never do the same.

Loss aversion is not just a cognitive and neurological phenomenon—how humans assess risk also has to do with their upbringing, culture, and current socio-political environment (see all of the Covid-19 pandemic!). But no matter what choices or situations we face, **we can always take charge and choose conscious action that aligns with our values and principles.**

- The **amygdala** is the part of the brain associated with automatic survival-serving functions, as well as knee-jerk emotional reactions. It focuses on loss and is risk-averse and fear driven.
- The **higher brain** regions such as the striatum and insula are where we process these reactions,

make predictions, and make calculations about
risk versus possible reward.

We might have an impulsive reaction to look at a
situation and think,

"That's too risky, no way!"

But it doesn't have to stop there.

Our higher brain can step in and notice this automatic
reaction. Being aware of our predisposition to
overinflate potential loss, we can choose to rationally
discount the fear signals coming from that part of our
brain.
*"Yes, there is some risk here, but it is not as much as
you think. Also, the potential rewards make it worth
the risk."*

People who have a lot of money and power can afford
to take more risks. And those from collectivist societies
similarly can take on more risk if they believe that
support from those around them can help offset that
risk. But perhaps the thing that most determines our
risk sensitivity is our own mindset.

To the extent that we are not mindful, not rational, and
not deliberate, our fear-based impulses will take over,
and we will be driven by loss aversion. We will indeed
be "safe," but we will probably not grow and develop,
and there will be opportunities we forfeit.

To the extent that we are conscious, rational, and
choosing how to respond to our first impulses, our
discipline and self-mastery will take over and guide our
lives. It may be scary to take on some risk, but we do so

in a calculated and balanced way, seizing opportunities and working constantly to grow, develop, and learn.

Challenging an inbuilt sense of loss aversion is first and foremost an exercise in being aware. Once you're aware of what you're doing, then you can:

- **Frame the situation differently**. You could say, "I stand to lose twenty dollars," or you could say, "I stand to gain twenty dollars," and each will change your focus.
  - Try framing the question or problem differently and put potential gains in the spotlight rather than dwelling on what could be lost.
- **Ask yourself whether loss, even if it does occur, is really all that bad.** It's not just focusing on loss that distorts our appraisals; it's our negative focus, i.e., thinking, "Losing twenty dollars is really, really bad, and I'd be so unhappy if it happened!"
  - Challenge this assumption and put loss into perspective. Is it really something you couldn't recover from?
- **Weigh things up.** Losses are painful, yes, but are you willing to pay that pain as the price of potentially accessing something a lot better? Every time you default to the status quo, you avoid potential risk. But you also forfeit any chance of the reward.
  - At least if you try, you have some chance of a good outcome. If you don't try, your chance of that good outcome is a 100% confirmed zero!
- **Be realistic about regret.** You might worry that you'll regret acting, forgetting that there is another potential risk—the regret of *not* acting.
  - It's trite, but "if you must be regretful, regret what you didn't do, not what you did."

TAKE ACTION: Right now, in your journal, write down five COSTS of keeping your life exactly the same as it is now. If you don't change in the least, what will you miss out on?
What will you regret?
What will never improve?

The Mere Exposure Effect

This is the cognitive bias wherein we develop a preference for something simply because we're already familiar with it—i.e., **"mere exposure" to something makes us tend to like it more.**

Sounds simple, but we really do tend to

- like the things we know.
- dislike the things we don't know.

It's easy to see why this may be a problem when it comes to self-discipline: It's a strategy optimized around *comfort* and *ease* rather than the best possible decision in each moment.

It's not rational, it's emotional.

You've probably experienced this effect in your own life countless times.

Example: Imagine you go to a restaurant serving a kind of food you're completely unfamiliar with. You look at the menu and have no idea what you're reading. You spot one dish that you're familiar with, and despite it being a distinctly boring and unadventurous choice, you choose it and forego trying something new and possibly way better.

There is an element of risk aversion, of course, but the bias is more or less,

"I like what I'm familiar with, and I don't like what I'm not familiar with."

This doesn't seem so bad, except that just like with loss aversion, we are not really making rational choices based on the merits of the options available to us.

Another example: We might keep buying a brand that is more expensive and lower quality simply because we've always bought that brand, and it's familiar to us. We have mistaken the warm-fuzzy feeling of familiarity for an objective appraisal of that option's good characteristics.

We may *feel* like we are happy with the choice we've made, but it's an illusion, and all we've done is:

- Narrow our perspective.
- Limit future decisions.
- Pass up opportunities that we may have derived more benefit from.

In other words, your new favorite food could be hiding in the pages of that menu, only you will never know it because you defaulted to the safe and familiar choice. Even worse, you may never even be aware of the absence of this delicious food in your life.

➜ There's no way around it: **The right option for you is not necessarily the most familiar one**.

In fact, the right option for you may currently be one *you don't even know about!*

Which means that to make that right decision, you need to get out of your comfort zone and go find it.

You will still be influenced by the mere exposure effect, but if you can increase the number of different ideas and options you expose yourself to, you are in effect making yourself more familiar with a wider range of possibilities.

The real problem with this cognitive bias is how invisible it is—and if you don't know something is happening, you can't fix or change it. For example:

- It's time for a vacation, but your stick-in-the-mud partner doesn't want to go somewhere they haven't been before. They ask you, "Can't we just go to the resort we went to last year?"
- A business is floundering, and independent consultants are brought in. But the bosses are adamant that, "If it ain't broke, don't fix it!" since they've been doing business this way for decades.
- A student submits a thesis, and the academics in charge find it too "out there." They reject it and ask the student to re-submit something more in line with the predominating school of thought in that department.
- Your cousin turns up to your party wearing a ruffled brown-and-fuchsia dress, plus Wellington boots. You instantly think, "I don't like that," when in reality, your true feelings are closer to, "Hm, I don't think I've ever seen you in anything like that before."

Any time we're in the realm of **stereotypes, automatic behaviors, peer pressure, assumption, and "tradition,"** then we are usually dealing with the false assumption that the familiar thing = the best thing.

We mistake a feeling of *comfort* and *predictability* with *liking*.

Again, there's an evolutionary reason for us being this way. Sticking with what we know reduces the threat of uncertainty and makes life simpler. Consider that it takes *cognitive effort* to process something new and different, and there's always an element of risk whenever something new comes along. Why change things up when what you have is working out okay?

The answer is: You've overestimated how well your current situation is actually working.

Familiarity and comfort are *not* a good basis for decision-making. Relying on them may seem to make life easier, but you forfeit something important in the process: your own self-determination.

It may not seem like it, but defaulting to the familiar choice weakens your self-discipline. It's the equivalent of shrugging your shoulders and choosing not to act. The result is that we could miss valuable opportunities, not to mention let our own autonomy and power of choice wither away.

We have to consciously increase our exposure.

- **Consciously choose novelty and variation,** even if it doesn't feel natural at first. Give every new stimulus or idea time to grow on you—try a new food a few times, or really listen to new concepts with an open mind before deciding you don't agree. Refuse to let initial discomfort scare you off—feeling unsure about something new is a natural reaction from your brain, but it's not helpful, so you can ignore it.
- **Embrace uncertainty.** Don't be in too much of a hurry to decide whether you like something or not, or whether it's good or bad. See how long you can stay in neutral "observer mode" and simply

gather information. You don't always have to arrive at a conclusion.

- **Remind yourself that neutral is not bad**. There is value in expanding your perspective and trying new things even if they don't turn out to be particularly pleasant. So, when you try something new, don't worry if it's not totally amazing. It's okay for it to be neutral—that's not the same as it being a bad thing.
- **Actively seek out things that oppose your status quo**. It may seem scary, but remember that you're still in control. Genuinely entertain opposing opinions (not just strawman arguments!) and be honest about the ways your present position can be improved upon. The people who learn the most in life are those who are not afraid to test their assumptions and challenge their pet theories.

TAKE ACTION: For one week, try to do something new and unfamiliar every day. It doesn't matter what it is, only it should be different in some way from your normal routine.

The Dunning-Kruger Effect Makes You Overestimate Your Abilities

When it comes to the roadblocks that get in the way of developing proper self-mastery and discipline, the final cognitive bias we'll consider is the Dunning-Kruger (DK) effect.

The DK effect is when a person lacks ability in a certain area yet still believes they are fully competent to give opinions or perform duties in

that subject... even when objective metrics or others may disagree.

Basically, it's a form of *double* ignorance—i.e., not knowing but also not knowing that you don't know. The corollary is that while people with less competence tend to overestimate their skills, great achievers tend to underestimate them. In fact, their more accurate assessment of their ability is itself a reflection of their competence—*they are smart enough to know how smart they are.*

You've probably seen this effect in real life:

- Someone may have learned about a new theory, idea, or technique a mere month ago, but now behaves as though they are the world's leading expert on that topic.
- They then get into a conversation with someone who genuinely *is* an expert in that area.
- But because the expert understands how truly complex the issues at hand are, they refrain from making bold pronouncements... leaving the first person plenty of opportunity to loudly explain it to them.

It's a decidedly awkward bias, but it happens—and though we don't want to admit it, it happens to *us*, too.

The phenomenon was first identified by Justin Kruger and David Dunning, who observed that the **ability and the confidence in one's ability often seemed inversely proportional.**

It makes sense that a person who lacks knowledge or understanding may also lack one crucial piece of knowledge and understanding—the accurate assessment of how much they really know.

In Kruger and Dunning's original research in the nineties, participants were assessed objectively on skills like humor, logic, and grammar. Then, they were asked to assess their own competencies.

- Those who scored lowest on the objective tests tended to greatly *overestimate* their performance.
- Those with the highest objective scores actually *underestimated* their own abilities.
- What's more, the *greatest* overestimations were by people with the *lowest* objective scores. Ouch.

Why does this happen? A few possible reasons:

- Plain old lack of insight and self-knowledge.
- The presence of a cognitive blind spot—you can't feasibly know what you don't know.
- Actively rejecting feedback and teaching, which means you never learn better and so your ability stays exactly where it is.

The DK effect can be devastating and is another cognitive bias that can wreak havoc—so long as you don't know it's there.

On a personal level, being badly inaccurate about your own abilities is an obvious personal handicap, but what about when a doctor greatly overestimates his ability? Or a business leader who holds the livelihoods of dozens of people in his hands?

Before you assume that the DK effect is the blight of the stupid, it's worth noting that *it's more about lack of insight than it is about raw intelligence.* In fact, a person who is extremely competent in one area of life may even more stubbornly cling to the idea that they automatically know about *all* areas of life, and behave accordingly.

"Intellectual humility" is something we all could do with more of. It takes self-discipline to accept that we may not be right about something, and that we may not be especially competent in an area.

→ **To be intellectually humble means we place true knowledge and understanding as our goal, instead of pride or the flattery of our egos.**

If we can be more intellectually humble, then we can cultivate more self-discipline and a more sophisticated sense of self-knowledge. But it's a virtuous cycle:

- The more self-discipline we have, the higher the standard we hold ourselves to.
- The higher our standards, the more intellectually humble we can be.

TAKE ACTION: It can be difficult to see all the ways you currently don't see, but whenever you're making decisions or weighing up choices, consider the following:

Don't Assume You Are the Best Evaluator of Your Own Abilities

Take your subjective assessment out of things and ask others for their input and feedback or find a way to measure your competence objectively.

Example: You can just make the assumption that, "I'm in great shape!" but how do you know? Instead:

- Go to a gym and get a full and comprehensive fitness test
- Get a physical exam at your doctor's

- Gather real, objective data to work with, such as your weight, resting heart rate, and body fat percentage

Don't Assume the Right Answer Will Always Come Quickly

We can blame certain cultural depictions of genius in the media for the assumption that experts know how to do things automatically and without effort.

This may make us believe that if we *feel* really certain about something, then we're likely more correct than if we're unsure, hesitant, or need to take time to process and analyze. But some things really do take time to figure out, no matter how competent or incompetent you are!

You don't have to go with your first snap decision.

Take your time to reflect.

Going with your first impulse is often a sign of a lack of discipline (as well as the mere exposure effect, or a simple emotional attempt to avert loss).

Example: If there's a problem to solve at work, you might be tempted to jump in and say,

> *"Oh, I know all about this problem! I'm an expert at this. Let me tell you how we should handle it."*

However, if you only pause and reflect for a moment, you may see the problem more clearly and give yourself time to genuinely process it. This is closer to how real experts handle a problem.

Don't Assume That It's Wrong to Not Have the Answers

It takes enormous discipline and self-awareness to be comfortable with your own limitations—much less to "admit" them!

Our egos can make us shortsighted and narrow in perspective. But this only happens if we have certain underlying beliefs, such as:

- It is better to know it all.
- It is preferable to be an expert than a beginner.
- Lacking answers or understanding is embarrassing.
- It is unacceptable to make a mistake.

In fact, a true expert has made more mistakes than an arrogant amateur will ever allow himself to. Comfortably embracing ignorance in the process of learning is what separates those with a so-called **"fixed mindset"** and those with a **"growth mindset"** (more on this later).

The latter are not afraid to ask questions or be wrong because they understand that this is the path to growth and learning.

- **A fixed mindset** convinces you that you already know it all, so you don't ask questions and you don't learn.
- **A growth mindset** *sees competence as something that can be gained and acquired—but in order to acquire it, you have to acknowledge that you don't yet have it!*

The best antidote to the DK effect is, in short, to not assume anything.

It is far more liberating to simply remain in ignorance, admit what you don't know, and adopt a mindset of ego-less curiosity. **One big impediment to overcoming the DK effect in your own life is believing that only other people suffer from it, and not you!**

It takes—you guessed it—self-discipline to continually hold yourself to a better standard.

Strengthen Your Metacognition by Asking for Feedback

Metacognition = the ability to think about your thinking.

When you attempt to foster self-discipline and self-mastery? That's you taking part in a form of metacognition.

Any time you reflect on your thoughts rather than merely *being influenced* by them, you open up a little window of opportunity where you can choose to act differently.

There is one concrete thing you can do to get the meta-cognition ball rolling when it comes to the DK effect: **Ask for feedback.**

- Ask a wide range of trustworthy people and be brave enough to take on board what they tell you.
- Ask neutral third parties at work for their opinion on your skills.
- Get task-specific feedback; for example, join a writer's group to share your work and see what other writers make of your work.

- You could even do a personality or intelligence test with a counselor to accurately pinpoint your strengths and weaknesses.

If you have to adjust your assessment of your competencies downward, don't see this as a failure. Congratulate yourself for being committed to genuine personal development and real self-knowledge instead of flattering illusions.

This is something to be genuinely proud of!

TAKE ACTION: Identify someone in your world who you can ask to give you feedback in the area you're trying to improve in.

Chapter Takeaways:

- By understanding potential roadblocks to better self-discipline, we can anticipate and prepare for them. The status quo bias is the preference for your current situation (even a bad situation) to remain the same, and it can prevent you from making necessary beneficial changes. Counter this by remembering that not choosing is also a choice.
- The sunk cost effect is another impediment; it's the increased tendency for people to continue with an endeavor if they've already spent time, money, or resources on it. It stems from lacking the insight that what has been spent is already gone—or sunk. Counter this by reflecting on the benefits of current and future possibilities, not on what cannot be changed in the past.
- Loss aversion is the cognitive bias that sees losses as more psychologically significant than gains of the same size, and also distorts our self-discipline. Make sure you're taking beneficial

risks by: re-wording the situation in terms of gain, not loss; downplaying the pain of loss; and re-framing the fear of future regret.

- The mere exposure effect is our predisposition to prefer familiar things, aka the familiarity principle. However, the right choice is not necessarily the one you've already been exposed to. Counter this by: increasing your exposure to other choices, embracing uncertainty, and seeking out novelty for its own sake.

Chapter 3: How to Develop Self-Discipline and Rock-Solid Focus

We've seen that self-discipline and self-control are all about delaying gratification and mastering your own limited willpower moment to moment. This constant tug-of-war is reflected in our neurochemistry, where our higher brain must learn to master and regulate our lower, more primal and fear-based brain.

We've also seen that there are sadly many cognitive biases that stand in the way of us fully developing our sense of self-control, including the sunk cost fallacy, the status quo bias, and loss aversion.

Now it's time to consider the methods available if we want to cultivate self-discipline *despite* these biases. Luckily, developing mastery over yourself is simply a matter of two things:

1.   Persistence
2.   Practice

Even if you are not currently a very disciplined or focused person... **you can be**. It's a choice.

We'll start in a very practical way: with daily habits.

Your habits are a reflection of your character.
And your character will help you reinforce the optimal habits.

Having looked at everything that can go wrong, let's consider what it looks like when it goes right and a person lives a self-disciplined life.

<u>The Daily Habits of the Self-Disciplined Person</u>

Disciplined and focused people may all choose to do very different things with their lives, but the **way** they do those things is generally the same. Jason Van Camp is the founder of Mission 6 Zero, which is a group specializing in performance enhancement. The team have consistently identified the *seven characteristics* unique to self-disciplined people, and these characteristics are expressed in their everyday habits:

1.   **They treat their bodies well.**

Willpower has a neurological basis.

Your brain is an organ, and it's a part of your body. If you are not eating well, sleeping enough, and staying fit and strong, it's almost impossible to exercise control over yourself mentally and emotionally, or achieve what you want to.

➜   Maintaining a wholesome and healthy lifestyle takes discipline, yes—but it also makes self-discipline so much easier!

You know the drill:

- Have a consistent sleep schedule with at least eight quality hours
- Eat a balanced, unprocessed, and nutritious diet
- Actively manage stress
- Prioritize physical activity with strength training, cardio, and flexibility practice

If you can commit to doing right by your health, it is an act of self-respect, which will boost your self-esteem and encourage you to hold higher standards for yourself in all areas of life. If you lack knowledge, then seek help. Hire a personal trainer, a therapist, a nutritionist, or even a personal stylist.

2.   They stay away from temptation.

Let's be honest—we live in a culture that constantly encourages us to have whatever we want whenever we want it. We have all come to internalize the idea that satisfaction and fulfilment are the same as having our desires instantly met.

Nothing could be further from the truth!

Self-disciplined people understand that they *cannot* have everything they desire in every fleeting moment. They don't put themselves in temptation's way, and they have a very pragmatic understanding of their own limitations.

➡ The idea is that if you control yourself in small, pre-emptive ways, you don't have to exert gargantuan efforts later on to rein yourself in.

You're on a diet? Don't go to the doughnut festival with your friend. Easy.

3.   They break things down.

A big goal is intimidating, but a small one isn't.

And every big goal is just a series of smaller goals.

Feeling intimated by a grand project that requires commitment and hard work? That's normal, no matter who you are.

- Some people will focus on the enormity of the task and be scared off.
- Other people will ask, "What small thing can I start with? How can I break this down into more manageable chunks? If I can't do this, what *can* I do?"

The thing is, if you have the discipline to perform a habit every day, consistently, for years, you actually can achieve those enormous goals. Just not all at once.

You don't have to say yes to the enormous goal—*just say yes to the next tiny step you have to do that day.*

That's all.

Then once you do that, do it again tomorrow. Then keep going.

4.   They proactively plan their routine.

Jim Rohn once said,

"If you don't design your own life plan, chances are you'll fall into someone else's plan. And guess what they have planned for you? Not much."

If you wake up and have no set routine in place, what determines what happens to you?

- Random chance
- Momentum
- Blind habit
- Other people's will

Sad to say, most people's biggest dreams and goals are not going to happen for them by sheer accident.

You've probably seen people recommend having a certain morning routine or how all the world's greatest leaders wake up at a particular time. But the exact routine itself is not important—what's important is that self-disciplined people take conscious control of their own time and plan it according to their will. This may mean waking up at 5 a.m., but not necessarily.

5. They understand the power of accountability.

Nothing is more common in this world than a person who blames someone or something else for their shortcomings.

It's the government.
It's your parents.
It's "society."
It's the weather.
It's the Illuminati again.
It's rude people in shops.
It's your bad knee.

Everyone is to blame but *you*.

Putting the fault on others feels like a relief because you are absolved of responsibility. But so long as you don't have that responsibility, you also give away something else: **your power to change.**

Self-disciplined people hold themselves to a higher standard and refuse to let excuses and blame take away their power.

- They don't see self-discipline as a horrid form of masochism.
- They don't see it as a punishment inflicted on them from the inside.
- Instead, they see it for what it clearly is: A gift and the freedom to live your life on your own terms.

Why would you want to give that power to someone else?

Sometimes it's easier to blame someone in charge than to **be** someone in charge, right? But the most self-disciplined know that a brutal kind of honesty is required: In the end, you are the one responsible for your life, and nobody else is coming along to sort it out for you.

6.   They have priorities.

Think of the people in your world who you admire for their self-discipline. You'll probably notice that whatever they're successful at, there are always some things they're *not* successful at because those things are just not their priority.

We are all mortal. That means that none of us have infinite:

- Energy
- Attention
- Intelligence
- Money
- Time
- Power

We have to budget what we have by choosing *the most important thing* and putting everything else second.

➜ You can do *anything* you want to.
➜ But you can't do *everything* you want to.

Disciplined people know that they need focus to decide what to pour their energy into.

7. They have clear vision

Being disciplined is one thing, but to what end?
Why be disciplined?
For what purpose?

The most self-disciplined people are not working hard and maintaining self-control for its own sake. They are not valiantly trying to emulate some impressive entrepreneurs they read about in the news just because it looks cool.

Rather, they are working hard *for something.*

They have a vision on the horizon that they can see, and they are working toward that. It's this vision that gives them energy, determination, resilience, and commitment.

BE AWARE: Be honest and ask yourself how well defined your goals are—if you have defined them at all. How focused have you been? Are your values and principles clearly guiding you toward a crystal-clear end point that you want more than anything?

If not, it's going to be hard to find the will to be as self-disciplined as possible.

To sum up, it's no good saying, "I want to be more disciplined," while at the same time eating loads of junk food, blaming others, and being unable to hold yourself accountable to any one goal or vision.

Again: The self-disciplined realize that nothing happens by accident—*it happens because we make it happen.*

TAKE ACTION: In your journal, note down the schedule you follow for your average day. Spend some time looking at how you spend time! Count how many hours you spend on sleep, on work, on self-care, on hobbies, etc.

Then express that as a fraction of the total day—for example, spending eight hours working means you give 8/24 hours a day working, i.e., 33% of your life working. Be honest and look at preceding weeks to see how every last minute of your time is spent.

What patterns do you notice?

Manage Your Energy, Not Your Time

What's the difference between time and energy?

Without delving into physics or philosophy, we can say that for ordinary human beings:

- **Time** is a limited or finite resource.
- **Energy** is something that can be refreshed and renewed.

No matter who you are or what you're doing, the quantity between noon and 1 o'clock is one hour, and that's that. But human energy can be expanded, regenerated, and cultivated.

Human beings derive their energy, or their ability to work, from their bodies, their emotions, their minds, and their spirits. While time passes by at a fixed and unchanging rate, energy is something you have far more control over.

In the realm of self-discipline, learning to budget your own internal reserve of energy may be one of the most powerful skills you develop.

Example: Jeff sits in bed in the evenings and scrolls through his phone, looking at junk he doesn't care about, until his eyes are sore and strained. He figures this isn't too bad a habit because he only does it for ten minutes or so and then goes to sleep. What's ten minutes, right?

But in focusing only on the time spent, Jeff is missing the *energetic cost* of this behavior. Although it's just ten minutes, this habit is:

- Damaging his eyesight
- Ruining his mood
- Wrecking his posture
- Undermining his sense of self-discipline

- And worst of all, setting him up for a night of poor sleep and consequently a groggy morning and a headache the next day.

Jeff could easily spend half as much time doing something else—like a relaxing ritual—before bed that could completely change everything. But he won't be able to do so until he shifts his focus from *managing time* to *managing energy.*

Let's consider again the four main areas where human beings are able to derive energy:

1. <u>From the body, i.e., the source of energy</u>

When your...

- Nutrition
- Exercise
- Sleep

...are all as they should be, **your physical body can become a source of renewable energy** that you get to tap into every morning when you wake up.

In fact, physical energy can be seen as the bedrock of the other energy types—it's way more difficult to be emotionally strong or cognitively sharp if your body is too weak to generate the energy needed.

Yet how many of us behave as if the exact opposite were true? We'll skip breakfast so we can rush to work, or say we're too tired to exercise... not realizing that a big part of our tiredness is *because* we don't exercise or eat well.

Dismissing your body's physical needs is a kind of slow suicide since everything comes to a grinding halt if your body is not healthy and strong.

TAKE ACTION: Right now, see if you can identify three physical habits and behaviors that are sapping your energy rather than supporting or regenerating it.

Ask what you can do to help your physical body *renew* its energy each day instead—don't just expect your body to support you no matter what punishment you throw at it!

2.   <u>From the emotions, i.e., the quality of energy</u>

If your body generates a fresh store of energy every day, it is the emotions that add color and dimension to this energy, i.e., **the body supplies the quantity and your emotions supply the quality.**

Broadly, what does life feel like for you?

- Positive?
- Negative?
- Anxious and fearful?
- Sad and depleted?
- Angry?
- Calm and content?

Your emotions act like a *filter* over everything. You may have a lot of energy, but if all that energy is colored by negative emotions, it doesn't quite matter! Luckily, we can consciously shape our state of mind and make efforts to influence the quality of our experience, i.e., how we feel.

You might be in peak physical condition but start every morning with a fight with your kids or partner, followed by a stressful train commute in which you scroll through doom and gloom news stories on your phone.

Even while you're properly managing your time and money, *you are not managing your emotions*, so you're losing all that power, vitality, and energy you generate by having a healthy lifestyle.

TAKE ACTION: Throughout today, as often as you can, become aware of your emotional state by simply pausing, breathing slowly, and checking in with your body and mind.

The first task is just to notice the quality of your emotional experience.

The second task is to see if you can locate this in your body. Just for a moment, see if you can consciously *choose* a positive frame of mind. Breathe deeply, relax your jaw, and let tension go.

We'll be looking at many different techniques for becoming aware, challenging old narratives, and beating stress, but for now, just acknowledge your power, in that moment, to steer your emotional reaction to things.

3.   <u>From the mind, i.e., the focus of your energy</u>

How many of us use our minds merely as self-torture devices?

How many of us truly understand that the mind is a tool, our tool, and use it for its real purpose, which is to help us focus our energy and bring our goals to life?

With a calm and positive emotional foundation, we can free our mind from fear and anger and distraction and **use its powers for good**. You'll already know how impossible it is to summon concentrated attention when you're tired, sad, or distracted.

➜ Imagine that your mind is like a powerful horse—once it's happy and well fed, it becomes a vehicle that you can hop on and steer, letting it take you more quickly to where you want to be.

When our minds are harnessed like this, we can focus and direct our energy whenever we plan, strategize, make schedules, or deliberately take charge of resources like time and money to achieve our goals.

This is the level where most business coaches and productivity experts focus on—but without appreciating the levels beneath it, all the tips and tricks in the world will be merely nice hypotheticals.

TAKE ACTION: When you're feeling physically strong as well as positive and calm, *then* is the time to put in place habits, plans, and schedules that you will be able to follow automatically later on, even in times when you have less energy. Start a habit of writing out your to-do list for the day in the morning, when you're most fresh.

Simple example: When you're feeling strong and energized, prepare healthy meals and freeze them. Later, when you're tired (low physical energy) and a bit grumpy (low emotional energy), you reach into the freezer and automatically make the right decision.

4. <u>From the spirit, i.e., the energy of meaning and purpose</u>

Finally, all human beings derive energy from the fact of knowing that their life serves some ultimate purpose, and that their actions are part of something bigger than themselves.

Without spiritual energy, life can quickly feel pointless and empty.

Your spiritual energy can come from

- Your sense of higher purpose
- Your values and principles
- Your deeply held convictions
- A feeling of connectedness to a greater cause

Many people do everything right but find they still lack self-discipline because deep down, something is not connecting for them on this level.

On the other hand, even someone with poor health, low mood, and weak attention can be energized by a sense of purpose if it's powerful enough.

TAKE ACTION: If you feel that you're ticking all the self-discipline boxes but still feel uninspired, it might be time to start asking some higher-order questions:

- What do you want to be remembered for in this life?
- What purpose do you think you were put on this earth to achieve, and how does your current task play into that?
- Who or what do you ultimately serve?
- What are the things that feed your soul and give you direction and courage? Are you connected to those things? If not, why not?

So, to sum up:

Your body supplies your life force.

Your emotions give that life force color and dimension.

Your mind helps you focus your efforts toward some goal.

Your spirit, finally, answers the biggest question: **Why** that goal? What is the ultimate point of having all this energy and focusing it in this way or that way? To what end?

A fully developed and self-disciplined person tends to know how to work with *all these energetic levels*.

To know how to shuffle around your time on a schedule or keep track of money is only one very small part of the puzzle. To conclude, here are a few ways to become better at managing your energy so that you are cultivating self-mastery over your *full* experience of life:

- **Work with your circadian rhythms.** Don't fight against your biological clock, but work with it. Plan the most important tasks for when you're freshest and most alert.
- **Rest.** Understand that whatever form of energy it is, it will need to be refreshed and reset periodically. Give yourself enough physical, emotional, mental, and spiritual rest when you need it.
- **Be a dynamic and varied person** and diversify your experience. You are a complete and three-dimensional being, so expose yourself to many different stimuli. When you plan your schedule, mix up physical exercise with mental effort and make space for emotional and spiritual engagement. Being one dimensional means being ineffective.
- That said, **don't multitask.** When you're doing something, do it. If you're taking a walk in the woods, do that with all five senses and without thinking about your email inbox! When you're at work, focus on the thing in front of you and guard your attention against distractions.

- If you're still trying to master energy regulation, you may need to try a **"screen detox"** or a fast where you cut down on distractions, temptations, and the general noisiness of life. Sometimes, reconnecting to your body, to nature, or to other people is all that's needed to refresh your inbuilt sense of purpose and self-discipline.

What It Means to Live Your Values

It does not matter what your values are.
What matters is how well aligned your life is to those values.

In other words, it is not the value that saves or redeems you, but rather your ability to *let that value guide you*, shape your behavior, and provide meaning to your life. It's no secret that people who have impressive self-discipline usually got that way because they know their values and they're actively living by them.

Knowing your values is extremely important, and yet it's work that nobody else can do on your behalf. There are two challenges:

1. Knowing your true values.
2. Knowing how to reflect these values in your life.

If your life is not currently feeling happy, focused, meaningful, or fulfilled, that's a good sign that one or both of the above challenges are not being met.

BE AWARE: Could you immediately and without hesitation answer the question, "What do you value?" if asked right now?

People have all sorts of values:

- Creating a loving and stable family
- Expanding knowledge and developing intellect
- Creating beautiful things or exploring the artistic and expressive realms
- Living a life of service to others
- Financial and material stability
- Being independent and autonomous; finding your true self
- Spiritual peace and connection
- Wisdom and contentment
- Excitement, fun, adventure, and novelty
- Power and influence
- Mastery over the physical body
- Friendship, loyalty, compassion, and social connection

Values are not something you choose or decide upon—they are something you discover.

They have to authentically speak to you and what matters to you. This means you cannot simply choose something that you think you *should* choose, or look to others and try to live your life according to their principles.

Finding your values is work only you can do, and crucially, your values may change over time, some becoming more refined, others being replaced or re-thought, and still others being shifted in their relative importance.

Ask yourself:

- Where have you always felt passion and energy in life? What has always gotten you fired up?
- When you have felt energized and "on purpose," what were you doing? What end were you serving?
- What was the first thing you wanted to do as a child?
- What kinds of people do you most admire, and why?

It may take time to answer these questions, but once you have, your challenge is to figure out how to **build a life that reflects them.** If you can do this, you have already achieved the lion's share of self-discipline—you have a "big why" that will supply you with more inspiration, motivation, and resilience than any salary, coercion, or social pressure ever will.

The idea is that when a person is living in alignment, life runs more smoothly—just like a car does when all its wheels are in alignment and pulling in the same direction!

TAKE ACTION: Look again at the schedule you wrote in the last section and compare it against the values you've discovered for yourself. Do your daily activities reflect your values? If you value family more than anything else, is that shown in the percentage of time you spend on those activities?

Self-discipline, then, is about the effort you spend to find your true north and keep pointing toward it. Self-discipline spent on working toward things you don't actually care about will always fizzle away with time whether you have discipline or not.

The difficulty with living your values is that it sometimes necessitates big, scary changes. Maybe you realize that your life lacks discipline and focus because you've been working for years in an industry that means nothing to you, while your true talent and desire goes un-nurtured and unfulfilled. You don't really lack discipline at all—what you lack is a worthy cause to discipline yourself toward!

Making changes to your life so that it more accurately reflects what you really value can take time, patience, and courage. Maybe you can't quit your job, move to a different country, or divorce your spouse just yet. But what you *can* do is make continuous baby steps in the right direction.

➔ Ask yourself regularly: **How would I act if I was living according to my values?** Then do that.

The next time you're faced with a decision, ask the above question, then choose how you would choose if you were someone who values what you value.

- Procrastinating?
- Dealing with conflict?
- Navigating change?

Then ask the question again. What would a person living their best, most authentic life do? How would they face this challenge?

Be patient—if you have never paid attention to your values before, it may take a long time to gradually rebuild a life according to completely different priorities. But you can draw energy and motivation from the fact that **no matter where you are, you can**

always take a small action in the right direction, right now.

Three Steps to a Values Upgrade

Step 1: Evaluate your lifestyle, but without judgment and negativity

If you are not spending time in a way that reflects your values, it's time to make changes. Track your behavior and compare it against the ideal, but stay away from blame, shame, and regret.

You'll experience some cognitive dissonance when you see *what is* and compare it to what *could be*, but don't get caught into thinking you're being hypocritical. Be patient, remind yourself of what's important, and keep taking inspired action.

Step 2: Instill new habits and forget about quantum leaps

You might be able to imagine a new life for yourself in two seconds, but it will take a lot longer than that to bring that vision to reality! What will get you there is not an overnight transformation, but the slow, consistent magic of a good habit. Don't try to do it all at once. Instead, ask: "What's the smallest thing I can commit to *every day*?" Smaller steps, if done diligently, will get you there faster than one impressive leap (which is impossible, anyway).

Step 3: Be willing to be in process

One big part of developing self-discipline, especially the self-discipline needed to change your entire life, is to understand that nothing worthwhile happens quickly.

Be patient. It takes time to grow and develop, so enjoy the process and don't be too quick to resolve issues or rush to find answers.

There will be some time when you're unsure of yourself, but you will gain mastery if you're patient and consistent. Your biggest threat is not that you won't improve, but that you will give up before having the chance to enjoy your improvement.

Be patient, and the changes *will* come.

TAKE ACTION: What tiny action can you take right now that is in the direction of your values?

Control Your Neurotransmitters—Don't Let Them Control You

A place where your physical, mental, emotional, and even spiritual energies collide is in the brain with your neurotransmitters. These are chemical messengers that enable neurons to connect and communicate with one another, and they have an astonishing degree of influence over every area of your life.

The relationship, luckily, goes both ways, and we also have a degree of control over our neurotransmitter balance—if we choose to exercise that control, that is.

➔ **We can recognize symptoms that our brain chemistry is out of whack and take conscious action to rectify that imbalance in a variety of ways.**

When we talk about neurochemical balance, we are not saying that behavior, emotions, society, or spiritual life don't matter—rather, we are merely looking at these very same phenomena, just on a different level.

Your brain is constantly trying to maintain chemical *homeostasis*, and the extent to which it can do this is the extent to which you will feel:

- Mentally resilient
- Content
- In control
- Able to focus

Poor equilibrium is associated with mental illness, addiction, or even conditions like epilepsy and Alzheimer's. When **serotonin**, **dopamine**, **acetylcholine**, and **GAMA** are imbalanced, so, too, will be your **behavior**, **emotional state**, and **cognition**.

Diet, as always, plays a big role in overall well-being and also supports brain health. After all, the molecules and electrochemical signals that make up your state of mind are ultimately made out of materials that come from the food you eat. There are no magical "brain foods" because your brain needs a spectrum of nutrition, just like the rest of you.

- Enjoy plenty of good-quality fats and omega-3s.
- Eat enough carbohydrates for energy, and maintain a stable blood sugar level, i.e., avoid fasting and binging.
- Steer clear of medications and drugs that destabilize your brain's delicate chemistry.
  - Amphetamines, benzodiazepines, and addictive drugs like cocaine can understandably shatter the physiological basis of solid self-discipline.
- Moderate or eliminate alcohol and nicotine, as well as processed foods and the deadly sugar-fat

combinations in most junk foods that are engineered to be addictive yet nutritionally empty.

Chronic stress disrupts brain homeostasis, too. Tension and anxiety are not free-floating abstract quantities—they are reflected in the body as stress hormones that have real and damaging effects via the HPA (hypothalamus, pituitary, and adrenals) axis.

Here's a quick rundown on your brain's neurotransmitters and how you can support them:

Serotonin

Signs you might have low serotonin:

- Binge eating, particularly carb cravings
- Low libido
- Low self-esteem and negativity
- Insomnia
- Hypervigilance
- Poor digestion

To balance serotonin, try:

- Eating more protein rich foods
- Eating protein and carbohydrates separately
- Taking tryptophan, magnesium, B vitamins, or omega-3 supplements
- Exercise, good sleep, and enough sun exposure

Dopamine

Signs you may have low dopamine:

- Low motivation, drive, or focus
- Apathy
- Addiction and compulsive behavior
- Anhedonia—not feeling much pleasure in anything

- Low zest, low libido, low energy

To balance dopamine, try:

- Foods rich in tyrosine, such as coffee and green tea
- Breaking down goals into smaller ones, rewarding yourself each time you achieve them
- Doing a "digital detox" (going offline or reducing screen time for a few days) to reset your reward circuitry

Acetylcholine

Signs you may have low acetylcholine:

- Poor memory, trouble finding the right words
- Lack of focus, lack of attention
- Brain fog

To balance acetylcholine, try:

- Eating more quality fats in the diet
- Ginseng supplements
- Reducing distractions in the environment
- Better quality sleep

GABA

Signs you may have low GABA:

- Constantly feeling switched on and wired
- Insomnia
- Palpitations, shortness of breath, sweaty hands
- Anxiety

To balance GABA, try:

- Eating a rich and varied diet with lots of fruits and vegetables
- Avoiding alcohol or drugs to relax
- Eating fermented foods

- Supplementing with taurine

Some people get their neurotransmitter levels checked and measured by a doctor and then take targeted supplements to support their neural health, but this is seldom necessary for ordinary people.

We don't need to have a degree in neurochemistry to know how to support our brains with healthy habits. But it *is* worth understanding the neurochemical basis for your thoughts, feelings, and behaviors, though, because it empowers you to take concrete steps to support yourself.

Feeling sluggish and unmotivated? It might not be a question of bad character. You may have simply depleted certain neurotransmitters in your brain.

Possible solution: What's needed is not more willpower, but a snack and a nap!

Feeling sad or angry? Before embarking on complex psychological explanations, consider first that you may simply be serotonin deficient.

Possible solution: more vegetables, better hydration or extra physical activity.

These concepts can seem painfully obvious, but the truth is that most of us take the physiological health of our body—and by extension, our brain—for granted.

We wrestle with the problem of our low self-discipline and try to implement complicated productivity techniques when all that was needed was better "brain hygiene" and a few tweaks of the diet.

TAKE ACTION: Time to clean up your diet. Look at what you eat and make three small changes for the week ahead—for example, eating three portions of leafy greens, having breakfast when you usually skip it, or taking an omega-3 supplement. If you're confused, ask a doctor or nutritionist for more specific pointers.

Triggers: Know What You're Up Against

If there were never any temptations or triggers in life, there would be no need for self-discipline. But, as it is, **one of the best ways to strengthen your self-discipline is to "know your enemy" and be prepared for how you will respond.**

What are emotional triggers?

They can be:

- memories,
- items,
- situations,
- physical sensations,
- thoughts,
- words,
- people,

or pretty much *anything* that instigates negative emotions. Sometimes, emotional triggers come in cascades.

This change in feelings can be rapid and more intense than the stimulus would rationally warrant.

Example: You're all of a sudden in a terrible mood, but when you stop and think about it, you realize that while in a bar, someone was wearing a perfume that reminded you of an ex-girlfriend and all the painful memories and associations that came with that time of your life.

Before you knew it, you were ordering a double whiskey even though you'd told yourself you wanted to drink less. That simple scent caused a chain reaction of behaviors that ended up with you hungover on your sofa the next morning! Like so many others, your noble intentions for self-discipline were undermined by powerful emotional triggers—and this can happen without you ever being the wiser.

As with anything that threatens our developing self-discipline, **we gain control over unconscious forces when we become aware and make them conscious.**

➔ If we know what our triggers are, we can take steps to pre-empt them and prepare ourselves.

If we can understand the processes informing our behavior, we empower ourselves to go in there and make deliberate changes to that process.

TAKE ACTION: Identify your own triggers before they set you off. Here's a simple three-step guide for doing just that:

Step 1: Identify your automatic responses

- Big idea: It's difficult to spot a trigger directly, but far easier to see what happens *after* the trigger, then work your way back.
- A sure sign something has been triggered? The feeling of being *automatically emotionally overwhelmed.*

o   Example: If you notice yourself suddenly feeling really angry, anxious, sad, etc., there's a good chance you've been triggered.

- Another good clue is when your response to a situation seems *disproportionate*.

o   Example: You have a total meltdown in the car just because the traffic light turned red, or you burst into tears at a joke on a TV show.

Step 2: Retrace your steps to find the trigger

- Big idea: Without judgment or shame, try to do a little detective work and find out what came before this disproportionate response. A few things to keep in mind:

o   The association or cause-and-effect relationship don't always make sense, but this doesn't really matter.

o   Remember that a trigger can be literally anything, including your own thought, memory, or another separate feeling. This is why it can take time to unravel!

- Example: You may notice that you lost your temper at the traffic light shortly after having the thought, "I need to get to work on time," and that your anger is really a response to a deeper feeling of pressure surrounding your job and has nothing to do with the traffic light.

- Another example: You might realize that you're suddenly upset at something innocent in a movie because one of the actors reminds you of your father, and you haven't realized how much you've been worried about his health lately.

Step 3: Repeat

- Big idea: Once you've found the trigger, it's up to you to decide what you do with it.

- If you notice that a certain trigger always pushes you to engage in addictive behavior, feel bad, or act out in ways that you later regret, then it may be time to make some changes.
- Example: You may notice that you have a bad habit of reaching for chocolate and candy after dinner in the evenings, but when you look closer, you see that there's boredom and loneliness that regularly arrives at this time of evening.
  - The solution in this example requires pre-empting this feeling and making sure that you have good company or something to do after dinner every evening so you're not triggered into the behavior you're trying to avoid.
  - Taking it further, you may want to explore some of these emerging issues of loneliness with a therapist. Could you be making more efforts to date or make friends? Should you be putting yourself out there more? The interesting thing about learning your triggers is that it leads you to novel solutions you might not have considered before.
- The process is ongoing. Stay aware and be mindful of your reactions at all times, and you will soon see a whole hidden world beneath your actions—a world that, once you're aware of it, you get to take control of.

Remember that triggers can be *anything*:

- They can be big (major life changes) or small (walking past an ice cream shop or it being 4 o'clock).
- They can include conversations, dynamics, certain people, sensations (smells, songs, clothing), places, dates, or times of year.

- They can be external (someone commenting on your height) or internal (you thinking to yourself, "I hate how short I am").
- They can be physical (feeling too hot or being ill), emotional (feeling scared), mental (being overwhelmed by difficult tasks), social (going to a massive party), or even spiritual (having to deal with a loved one's death).
- A trigger can cause one behavior, which may then act as a trigger for *another* behavior, so be prepared to work through a few tangles!

The Self-Disciplined Life—Putting It All Together

Developing self-discipline, then, is not a single behavior or mindset, but rather a collection of consistent habits, attitudes, and ways of being that allow you to work alongside your limits.

Self-disciplined people credit many different things for their success and focus:

- A proper morning routine.
- Optimizing the first and the final hour of each day with journaling or meditation.
- A gratitude practice.
- Healthy eating, sleep, and exercise.
- Stress management.
- Goal setting in alignment with your values.
- Etc.

So, which of these should you start with on your path to becoming a more self-disciplined person? Which approach is *best*?

Hopefully, this chapter has shown you that **all** of these approaches can have benefit because they all increase self-awareness and self-mastery, whether that's on the physical, emotional, mental, social, or spiritual level. Because all these levels are connected, an improvement in one is automatically an improvement in another.

Let's look at a few examples to show how the self-disciplined life is a manifestation of **self-awareness** and **self-mastery** on all levels of experience.

Example 1

Carrie works for a big multinational company. By the age of 36, though, she's starting to burn out. She diagnoses her problem as a lack of self-discipline, telling herself that procrastinating at work, smoking too much, and neglecting her relationships are signs that she needs to control her impulses and work harder.

But where to start?

Using the information described in this chapter, she decides that for two whole months, she will focus exclusively on getting her *physical* energy up.

Without thinking about discipline, goals, or focus, **she simply works on constructing a healthy daily schedule that** she knows will set the right foundation:

- 6:30 – Wake up, stretch, have a quick walk outside in the fresh morning air.
- 7:00 – Breakfast of a vegetable omelet and black coffee, and a moment spent in prayer, journaling, or just contemplation before the day starts. Take vitamins. Get ready for work.

- 9:00 – Work, but with plenty of scheduled breaks and stretch periods, and lots of water and green tea.
- 12:00 – Lunch break: chicken salad, read a book, call a friend, or write in gratitude journal.
- 13:00 – Work, but with careful attention spent on removing distractions.
- 17:00 – Home time. Prepare a healthy dinner from scratch, thirty minutes of Pilates, and no more than an hour of TV or scrolling online. Family time. Lay out clothes for the next day and use journal to check in on the next day's goals.
- 10:00 – Start winding down for bed. Meditate, read, and sleep ritual to manage stress.

Carrie follows this plan for two months, making sure that every single day, she is eating well, sleeping properly, and enjoying physical exercise and wholesome social interactions.

Only *then* does she start to look at the rest of her life.

She notices that her lack of self-discipline was not the problem—it was the *symptom* of a problem, that problem being a poor lifestyle.

→ Carrie had been telling herself, "Let me first fix up my self-discipline issue, and then I'll make all those healthy choices," but in reality, making healthy choices was the very thing that allowed her to have self-discipline.

Example 2

On the other hand, consider Matt, who already has a great lifestyle and is extremely health conscious. He's also a personal development junkie and is constantly attending self-improvement seminars and reading books designed to improve his life. And yet he feels like he's constantly battling:

- laziness,
- procrastination, and a
- lack of motivation.

Clearly, he doesn't have the same problem as Carrie.

Instead, he focuses on *how* he's spending his energy and vitality.

Using mindfulness exercises, journaling, and some pointed questions, he realizes the problem: **He does not know what his values are and is operating without a clear sense of his higher purpose in life.** Consequently, he can't feel genuinely inspired by anything and keeps jumping around from one exciting thing to the next, losing interest quickly. His life has filled up with things that he thinks he should be interested in... but isn't.

After six months of delving deeply into his "big why," grounding himself spiritually and asking the hard questions about what really matters, he... finds himself in a worse position than before.

Why?

Because nothing in his life really speaks to this newly developed sense of meaning. Though others are impressed by it, his job now feels pointless. Though he has spent time building his investment portfolio, he realizes he had not given enough thought to what to **do** with all that money, and why.

There's a lot that needs to change!

But the good news is that for the first time in his life, he's actually inspired to make those changes.

→ The problem was not that Matt lacked self-discipline, but that he needed to do the difficult work of building a life that would make that self-discipline mean something.

Unlike Carrie, he had to make more fundamental changes.

This is why success can look so different for so many people, and why **there is no such thing as a one-size-fits-all solution**.

- For one person, "self-discipline" means the courage to work hard.
- For another, it means quitting a job and working *less*.
- For some, self-discipline means clinging more tightly to the single thing that matters most in life.
- For others, it's more about consciously letting go of distractions and diversions.

The self-disciplined person's life will always be three things:

1. Conscious
2. Controlled
3. Proactive

TAKE ACTION: Of all the concepts discussed so far, which one has appealed most strongly to you? Today, decide how you can start practically bringing that idea into your own life in your own way. Remember that baby steps are the most powerful.

Chapter Takeaways:

- Your habits are a reflection of your character, and your character will help you reinforce the optimal habits. Disciplined people tend to share the same daily habits, such as treating their bodies well, being accountable to their own vision and goals, avoiding temptation, planning, prioritizing, and, of course, taking conscious action.

- Self-disciplined people manage energy, not time. There are four sources of energy: the body, the emotions, the mind, and the spirit. Depending on where you're strong, you'll need to budget your energy to properly support your goals.

- Values are a source of self-discipline: What matters is how well aligned your life is to those values. Neutrally evaluate your current lifestyle and make baby steps toward creating a life that brings you closer in sync with your values.

- Neurotransmitters matter: We can recognize symptoms that our brain chemistry is out of whack and take conscious action to rectify that imbalance in a variety of ways. Whether it's serotonin, dopamine, or others, the usual remedy is a healthy diet.

- Be prepared for how you will respond to emotional triggers such as memories, situations, or people who instigate negative emotions. We gain control over unconscious forces when we make them conscious. Pay close attention to automatic or disproportionate emotional responses and examine their causes.

- Self-discipline is not a single behavior or mindset, but a collection of consistent habits, attitudes, and ways of being.

Chapter 4: The Rules for Effective Habit Building

In the previous chapter, we looked at how to set up what is basically self-discipline *scaffolding*:

- A healthy life
- Crystal-clear values and principles
- Enough awareness to recognize your triggers and proactively prepare to choose better anyway

Now, in this chapter, we'll be looking at *ways to build on this initial scaffold.*

That's because while a healthy lifestyle and a well-developed self-awareness is half the battle, it is only half the battle—at some point, you will face barriers, hurdles, and challenges that get in the way, no matter how good your daily routines and habits are.

Below are some practical tools to help you when that happens.

The 40% Rule and the Secret to Mental Toughness

The 40% rule is a principle that can help you push through when things get tough.

First coined by self-help author David Goggins, this rule is a quick way to get around self-limiting beliefs.

It goes like this:

> **When you are beginning to feel tired in both body and mind, you may feel like giving up, but in truth, *you are only at 40%* of what you are truly capable of achieving.**

Why would this happen?

Well, the boundary is something your own brain creates and not an objective fact about reality. Recall that primitive part of the brain, the brainstem, the primary function of which is to keep you safe. This instinctual part of your brain wants to protect you from uncomfortable and potentially dangerous situations—and it's always better to be more cautious than less cautious, right?

So, as a result, you may feel:

- Physically exhausted
- Mentally worn out
- Just plain scared (even when you are not really in any danger).

The 40% rule tells us something encouraging: Even though you feel all of the above, *you may still have 60% more effort to give!*

The gist is that **you are capable of much, much more than you think you are. Even when you genuinely feel too tired to carry on, you can recognize that this is just an excuse.**

➜ **You are NOT done; you are only 40% done.**

Your mind may know how to push all the right buttons.

It may be very convincing.

It can tell all the right stories and concoct countless reasons for why you absolutely cannot go any further.

But if you can see all this for what it is, you realize that *you actually have the choice to keep going and do more.*

Mental toughness, then, is not about being some kind of superhuman, but rather about having the ability to not take your word for it when your body and mind tell you, "I can't do more."

Your brain is powerful—so powerful that when it tells you, "You can't do more," then that's precisely what it believes. But what if you tell it, "You *can* do more"?

- In an interesting 2008 study published in the *European Journal of Neuroscience* (Pollo et al.), scientists gave one group of participants a placebo pill, telling them it was performance-enhancing caffeine.
- Another group got an actual caffeine pill but were not told it would help their performance.
- When both groups were asked to perform some weightlifting exercises, can you guess what happened? *It was the placebo group that lifted the most weight—not the caffeine group.*

That's a pretty big deal—it means that what the brain believes to be true is powerful enough to change the way that actual muscle tissue behaves, making it stronger and more resilient. **Your beliefs about your own abilities are about so much more than just your attitude—they have the capacity to literally change your body.**

At some point in your self-discipline journey, you will tell yourself, "I can't do this." But at that point you need to remember where this thought is coming from and have the presence of mind to say, "Thanks, brain. I know you're trying to help, but I can do more."

Disciplined people are not people who find hard work easier or more enjoyable. They find it just as challenging and uncomfortable as you do! The difference is, they know that **feeling a little hesitant, afraid, lazy, or tired is simply not a good enough reason to stop.**

The good news is that becoming mentally tough is, ironically, not as hard as you think it will be, and it is something you *can* do! Here's how.

- **Don't take your own word for it**. The next time you hear the thought, "I can't do this. I have to stop. I'm too tired/scared/not good enough, etc.," then be ready to respond immediately with a more positive alternative.
  - Counter that thought with, "You've got this" or "You are stronger than you think."
  - You don't have to believe it 100%, just make sure you're not letting that self-defeating thought go unchallenged.
- **Make friends with discomfort**. Nobody, absolutely nobody, achieves anything valuable

by staying firmly in their comfort zone and doing the easiest thing possible.

- o Don't wait for challenges to push you; instead, proactively expose yourself to the things you're scared of. Trust that going outside your comfort zone is only scary for a little while, and that you will gain mastery as you go.
- o Analogy: Getting into a pool can be icy cold at first, but if you take the plunge, you quickly enjoy the new temperature.
- **Remember your purpose.** Your values, principles, and higher vision for your life will give you the courage to push on when your brain is convincing you to quit.
- o Example: You may not be able to exercise hard for the sake of six-pack abs, but you *are* willing to do whatever it takes to stay healthy and be around to watch your grandkids grow up. So tap into that and keep going.
- **Know that action creates motivation, not the other way around**. Too many people think that they have to wait until they feel fired up and motivated to act. Guess what? They never act.
- o Instead, when you act (no matter how unready you feel), you actually create forward momentum and build your motivation.
- o Act *even if* it's imperfect action. Act *even if* you're not inspired to.
- **You can give up—later**. Here's a good trick to help you push on. When you're close to throwing in the towel, make a little deal with yourself. "You have full permission to give up, but just do a tiny bit more first, and *then* you can give up."
- o Something awesome happens—when you push just a little more, you discover that you are not in fact at the end of your resources. If you can do

just five minutes more, do them. You may find you're *wanting* to do five minutes more after that.

Whether you call it

- Grit
- Ambition
- Perseverance
- Self-discipline
- Mental toughness

...or something else, it all comes down to the ability to keep going *even if* you're tired, scared, or unmotivated.

The ability to do this is not as complicated as it seems: You simply recognize that you feeling like you're "done" is not, in fact, **the point at which you are genuinely done.**

You're just getting started.

BE AWARE: Have a look at an arbitrary limit you have set for yourself in life, for example, "I can't manage the ten-pound weights." Where did this thought even come from? Have you ever challenged it?

Demand More of Yourself With the 10X Rule

A related principle that will help you develop the kind of consistent habits needed for a disciplined life is called the 10X rule. There are two parts to the rule. Simply put, you should:

1) **Set goals for yourself that are *10X higher* than what you think, and**

2)   **Take actions that are *10X greater* than you think, to achieve those goals.**

When it comes to fulfilling your potential, one of your biggest drawbacks may not be lack of skill or resources, but **goals that are too small**.

Just as in the 40% rule, where we greatly overestimate how tired and incapable we are, the 10X rule tells us that we tend to set goals for ourselves that are far below what we are really able to accomplish. And even then, we may routinely put in far less work to achieve that goal than is really required.

➔   The idea is: huge goals, huge action.

The 10X rule was created by entrepreneur Grant Cardone and was the subject of his bestselling book by the same name. Cardone talks about the Principle of Massive Action, i.e., **if you put in exceptional amounts of effort into something, you're likely to get exceptional results back**. For Cardone, success is an important part of life (in fact, he sees it as your *duty*), and it's possible with the right mindset.

That same little voice inside that tells you "I can't" when, in fact, you've only done 40% of what you're capable of is the same little voice that argues against you reaching for your dreams and ambitions.

It tells you that working toward your dreams is impossible or pointless.

No, it's not about being a crazed success-hungry maniac—it's just about realizing that *you don't have to limit yourself.*

"Success" can mean everything from financial and material stability to education, family goals, and even spiritual development. Whatever it is you want,

Cardone says, **with 10X the effort, you can achieve more than you ever thought possible.**

Again, we see that fear and a fondness for the status quo keeps us playing small and working toward mediocre goals that don't really fire us up. We almost always choose targets that are too small, not too big. And then on top of that, we don't even fully apply ourselves to these targets, and so we drastically undermine ourselves and forfeit our potential.

Cardone has a few principles that hit at the heart of the mindset he believes we should all cultivate:

- Success is not an option but a duty.
- Instead of explaining away failure or making our goals smaller, we should make our action bigger.
- You are not a victim, you are the author of your life.
- Look at what is considered a normal level of effort and put in 10X as much effort toward your own goal.

Not all action is created equal.

- Some actions are just plain mediocre.
- Some actions keep you treading water.
- Some actions will take you backward.
- Some actions will propel you forward.

But the *only* kind to propel you forward is *massive action*. Here's are three things to keep in mind:

Chose ambitious goals – Ones where you are almost leaping out of bed in the morning because you're so energized to get them done. Make those goals clear, too. You want to be able to visualize what you want with so much clarity that you can almost taste it.

Be prepared – Automatically assume that to achieve your goals, you will need to put 10X as much effort in as you originally guessed, or 10X as much as people tell you you'll need. Take it as a given that you will need to work really, really hard.

Don't compete, don't compare – Your goal is never to do better than someone else, but to do the absolute best that *you* can do regardless of what others have done. Don't worry about following trends or imitating other successful people. Matching your effort to other people's reins in your own innate potential.

The 10X method can sound pretty in-your-face, but think of it as a powerful antidote to the negative bias we all tend to have, i.e. the on that tells us:

- Think small
- Hang back
- Expect less
- Hesitate
- Be cautious

In short, it tells us to *underestimate ourselves.*

How many of us are unconsciously limiting how much success or happiness we have in life?

How many of us are playing it safe and putting in only the bare minimum of effort required and quietly hoping that will be enough?

How many of us have agreed to diminish our goals or expect less of ourselves?

➜ The 10X rule is about challenging all this. ***It asks us to demand that we are better than average.***

Nobody else is coming to save you or to help you make your life successful—that's your job. If you approach everything you do with this attitude of responsibility and accountability, then you are naturally optimistic. You trust that deep down, you will figure things out, and this gives you the resilience of knowing that whatever it is, you can do it.

So, you don't wait around for permission from others or for the magical set of perfect conditions.

Just commit, then figure out the details as you go.

Too many people think that it's audacious or arrogant to dream big. They think, "Who am I to want all this for myself?" But then again, why shouldn't you? Who are you *not* to want big dreams?

What does the 10X rule actually look like in practice? Here are some examples.

- You have your own business and are growing steadily. But rather than getting complacent, you set some goals for the upcoming year. You originally decide you want to make 10% more, but on second thought, you challenge yourself to use the 10X rule—*why not aim for a 100% increase?*
  - When you think about it, **you realize that your previous goal wasn't a goal at all, but an unconscious and self-imposed limit**. It's a way to say, "Don't make more than 10% more next year."
  - You work hard and guess what? You don't reach your 100% goal. But you do make it to 70%. Would you have managed that if you had settled for the smaller goal?
- You are starting out as a photographer and have your eye on a few prizes and awards. You follow the 10X rule and fully prepare yourself for the

fact that **you will have to work 10X harder than you first believed.**

o   Your photographer tutor says, "Try to enter a competition every month to stay on top of your game." You decide to enter *ten* competitions.

•   You're in a weight training group and finding yourself improving steadily. You all join a local triathlon and start training. During training, you notice that you are in the top 10% of your group. This would be a great achievement in itself, but **who says other people should be the metric of your success?** Who says they should define what counts as your *absolute best*?

o   On the day of the triathlon, you tell yourself your goal is to finish *in the top* 1% of *all* the participants. This way, you haven't let success be the enemy of your continued improvement. Don't let middling successes stand in your way of bigger ones!

TAKE ACTION: Be honest with yourself and ask if the goals you have right now are mediocre. Are you playing it safe? In your journal, have the courage to write down a truly massive, audacious goal—go wild and think of something you want that gives you goosebumps.

One word of warning, however: It's a bad, bad idea to throw yourself into a goal that is not genuinely something that speaks to you. Investing 10X the effort into an enormous goal that doesn't actually relate to your values will mean one thing only—you burn out 10X as hard!

Be cautious not to fall into the trap of making an idol out of hard work and being relentless for its own sake. Too many overachievers and ultra-accomplished people are actually hiding a secret: Their motivation comes from a deep inner confusion and lack of focus.

In their case, staying busy and working hard is actually just a distraction from the *real* work of life. The real work? Maybe it's to:

- stop
- take a break
- change course
- ask a hard question
- or (gasp) admit you were wrong!

Don't work yourself to exhaustion because of the belief that you are worthless without it. A ruthless schedule can sometimes be a mask for poor self-esteem (i.e., negative self-talk framed as a motivational speech), and hard work becomes a masochistic punishment.

The way out of this trap?
Keep aligning with your **values**.

➜ Hard work itself is never the value. It's only the means to get to what you value.

Being a martyr, showing off, or being ultra-tough with yourself are not the goals. If you find yourself wanting to emulate a badass navy seal and beat your fists on your chest, ask yourself honestly if there's more difficult work you're avoiding.

Keep on Top of Tasks With the Ten-Minute Rule

The ten-minute rule is both a productivity trick and a way to push through procrastination. It's easy:

➜ **No item on your to-do list should take longer than ten minutes.**

If a task *does* take longer than ten minutes to do, then break it up into smaller tasks until it doesn't. That, or delegate the task to someone else or delete it entirely.

By doing so, you:

- Instantly bring more focus, speed, and efficiency to your day.
- Beat procrastination.
- Strengthen your self-discipline.

Everyone can manage to do something for just ten minutes at a time, right? It may seem crazy to suggest that you could do everything you need to do this way, but you can!

To use this rule, try to remember your options:

Delegate
To get more time in your day, better manage your energy, and save it for what matters, delegate.

Good boundaries mean you don't say yes to everything, but only to those things that are *essential* to your most important goal that day.

If it's not important? Then you have just two options:

1. Ditch it entirely
2. Get someone else to do it

This may mean having to let a few things slide or be done less than perfectly—but if they are not your priorities, so what?

You could delegate "down," but don't forget that you can also delegate "up," i.e., to superiors, supervisors, or people who actually know better than you. In other words, ask for help!

Start With the Low-Hanging Fruit

Yes, you should have big, hairy, audacious goals, and yes, you should be working hard, but sometimes if you're having trouble getting started, you can get the ball rolling by *starting with the easiest task first.*

Naturally, you want to avoid endless "research" or planning, but begin any task with those quick gains that can be made without too much effort. This will give you confidence to keep going.

➡   Tip: Sometimes, your easiest and most satisfying task might simply be breaking things down into smaller tasks—which is intrinsically rewarding because it makes you feel like the project is manageable.

Use a Timer

Use your phone to set a ten-minute timer, and when it goes off, stop what you're doing. You may wonder, "What if I'm genuinely not finished with my task when the timer goes off?" Well, there are a few things you can do:

- Notice exactly what task runs over time and notice if it repeatedly happens
- Ask if you need to plan this task better next time, or if the chunks need to be broken down further
- Look at the task again and see if you *really* need to continue
- Consider if the rest of the task can be delegated or assigned for later

This technique will eventually teach you to **cut to the chase quickly.**

If you are routinely not getting to the crux of each task within ten minutes, something is wrong. Either you are planning poorly, or you're wasting time with things that are actually not necessary.

The human attention span does not follow along neatly with the hours and half hours on a clock—ten minutes is actually plenty of time if you are consciously brining your full, fresh attention.

Keep Tabs on the Bigger Picture

Of course, nobody writes an essay or builds a house in ten minutes. But the technique can still be used for bigger tasks in that it will:

1. Help you overcome procrastination, and
2. Get you thinking clearly about the stages and steps of the process.

When you are unclear about what you're doing, you can waste enormous amounts of time. The clock may show that an hour has passed, but in reality? You've only mustered a few minutes of *quality* time during that period.

➜ Set the timer and work on the small chunk of the bigger task.

Then, when the timer goes off, pause and see where you are. You may be very surprised at just how much work can be accomplished in ten minutes!

And anyone can manage ten minutes of solid effort, even on a task they've been avoiding. Decide then if you want to set the timer for another ten minutes. You don't have to, but if you do, commit to that full ten minutes, **absolutely no excuses**.

This technique works for procrastination because it eases some of the main causes of procrastination:

1. We are overwhelmed with the size of the task. But if we do just ten minutes, we don't focus on the enormity of an intimidating task, just on the next ten minutes.
2. We have planned poorly and don't actually know the smaller steps in front of us or the broader outline of the task we're doing. Lack of clarity can lead to lack of motivation, and you may feel aimless and irritated. Having to break the task down into logical ten-minute chunks forces you to remove this obstacle and think strategically.

Focus on Output and Not Outcome

If you sit down to study a 10,000 word chapter in your textbook, and you focus on that enormous-sounding number—*10,000!*—then it's going to feel like heavy lifting.

- Focusing on the **outcome** almost always means looking far over the horizon at a goal that's really, really far away.
- But if you focus on the **output**, you pull your attention back to the only thing you have control over—your attention right now in this moment.

Just read one paragraph.

Try to understand that paragraph.

Make some notes.

Take a breath, go in again, and read the next paragraph.

Simple!

One way to think of this rule is even simpler still: **Just start.**

Very often, the most difficult part of a project is simply summoning up the momentum to get going. Once you've begun, you start to see what the next step is, and the next...

Before you know it, half an hour has passed and you've covered enormous ground.

In just the same way as your brain will trick you into thinking you're finished when you're only 40% finished, your brain will also convince you that the task ahead is very difficult, very boring, too complicated, totally unmanageable, etc.

When you just leap in and start, you short-circuit these excuses and **begin before you can talk yourself out of it!**

TAKE ACTION: Pick a task you've been putting off and identify the first ten-minute task you'll have to do to get the ball rolling. Without thinking too hard about it, set the timer and just start with it.

Ten minutes may not seem like much, but then again, an hour is only a few ten-minute chunks one after the other.

➔ Remember: The most complicated task in the world is similarly made up of very simple ones.

Even if you can only eke out ten minutes on a project before you stop again, well, that's great: The next time you start, the task is that little bit smaller than it was.

One final point to remember about this rule is that breaking things into chunks is intrinsically rewarding. **After each baby step, have a mini celebration.**

Tell your brain this is a reward so that it releases dopamine—a neurotransmitter that teaches you, "This is good. Do this again." With every completed baby step, you feel a teeny tiny pop of pride, and that's one small vote of confidence in your own abilities.

Control Your Breath, Control Your Life

Anxiety is a psychological phenomenon, but it has its roots in the body's physiological responses to stressful situations. Your body's response is in large part automatic, but that doesn't mean we can't exert some influence over it.

➔ **One way to control our physiological response to stress is to control our breathing.**
➔ **Breath control = arousal control.**

And if you can control your physiological arousal, you are able to have a high degree of self-mastery and discipline over your entire life, not just your body.

Example: Imagine you're about to walk into a make-or-break job interview. Your fight-or-flight mechanism is in full swing (hello again, primitive hindbrain!), and adrenaline is flooding your system, causing:

- a racing heart,
- tense muscles,
- rapid breathing,
- sweating, and
- a weird churning feeling in the pit of your stomach

All these physiological responses are mediated by the HPA axis, and this complex interplay between neurotransmitters and stress hormones creates an experience of anxiety.

The resulting *emotion* is fear.

The resulting *thought patterns* are likewise fearful.

Importantly, though, the influence is not just one way. **It is not just your body that impacts your emotions and thoughts. You can also influence your body by changing your emotions and thoughts.**

Now, the automatic fight-or-flight mechanism is *not* something you can control. You have no say over the stress hormones that are released or what your pituitary gland is doing. But there is one important thing you can control: *your breathing.*

Calm this part of the system, and you can affect the rest of the system.

So-called **"box breathing"** is one way to do this:

1. Inhale slowly through your nose for a count of five, feeling your belly fill up.
2. Hold this breath for five counts.
3. Exhale slowly through your mouth for a count of five.
4. When you have emptied your lungs of air, hold for five counts.
5. Inhale slowly again.

You can try box breathing any time you notice your stress response getting out of hand.

Example: As you're waiting to be called into the interview room, you take a minute or two to slow down your breathing. In fact, you find that you can continue with deep breathing all through the interview, too, and this helps steady your speech and make you come across as calmer and more in control (because, well, you are!).

The human fear response is a wonderful thing. It evolved over thousands of years to help us stay safe and alert in the face of danger.

But again, we have also evolved a higher brain that can step in and tell us, "Actually, there isn't any real danger here, and this stress response is getting in the way."

A big part of true self-discipline is control over the self—especially in those moments when you feel out of control!

Even if you are in a dangerous situation, consciously taking control of your body by controlling your breath can help you be *more* effective.

You stop panicking.

You give yourself the opportunity to resolve issues swiftly and without losing your head.

Deep slow breathing is a way to take back control from an automatic knee-jerk response and turn it into something deliberate and conscious.

- If you're in a traffic jam that's making your blood boil, stop and take a few deep breaths.
- If you're getting overwhelmed at how much there is to do and feeling rushed and pressured, stop and take a few breaths.
- If you're in an emotionally charged conversation and can feel yourself getting upset, stop and take a few deep breaths.
- If you're feeling the rush of temptation beckoning you, stop and take a few deep breaths.

When you breathe more deeply, you are sending your body the message,

➜ **"My rational, calm self is now in control, and not my impulsive, instinctive self."**

Give yourself a few moments to let your heart rate slow and your breathing regulate itself. Feel the panic and emotion subside. Then, from *that* state of mind, decide on your next action.

- In the traffic jam, you choose not to lose your temper.
- Overwhelmed at work, you calmly ask what single task you should do next, then just focus on that.
- In a heavy conversation, you decide to hold your tongue and ask that you continue later when you've had time to compose yourself.
- Faced with a moment of strong temptation, you act quickly to remove yourself or choose an alternative (perhaps reminding yourself of the 40% rule!).

Having good habits and a healthy lifestyle go a long way to countering impulsivity, but sometimes you need a quick fix in the heat of the moment. You don't have to wait until an emergency, however!

Try deep breathing exercises throughout the day whether you're feeling overwhelmed or not. Try them:

- When you wake up
- When you go to sleep
- Before you head off on a journey
- At the start of every meal
- Every time you switch tasks

You can vary the breathing pattern, too.

Example: Pause for longer than five counts of five and gradually crease the length of breaths and pauses, which will help you get progressively calmer. The precise technique doesn't matter; what matters is that you are activating your higher mind, regaining control, and deliberately calming your automatic physiological stress response.

TAKE ACTION: Right now, as soon as you finish reading this chapter, try a few minutes of deep breathing. Feel your heart rate slow. Go quiet. No matter what has come before or what is coming next, relax. Then open your eyes and notice how you feel.

Chapter Takeaways:

- Habits build self-discipline. One great habit is the 40% rule, which says that when you're beginning to feel tired and ready to give up, in truth, you are only at 40% of what you are truly capable of achieving—so push through. Embrace discomfort and let your higher purpose help you be mentally tough.
- Also use the 10X rule, which says you should 1) set goals for yourself that are 10X higher than what you think, and 2) take actions that are 10X greater than you think, to achieve that goal. Be ambitious and don't settle for mediocre goals—but also refrain from comparison to others.
- The ten-minute rule is easy: No item on your to-do list should take longer than ten minutes. Achieve this by delegating, breaking tasks into smaller chunks, beginning any project with the easiest tasks first, using a timer, tuning in to the bigger picture, and focusing on your process rather than the outcome.
- Finally, one way to control our physiological response to stress is to control our breathing. Breath control is arousal control.

- Use box breathing to calm your nervous system, and tell yourself, "My rational, calm self is now in control, and not my impulsive, instinctive self."

Chapter 5: Avoid These Self-Discipline Traps

Self-discipline is cultivated over time. Expect that you will have setbacks. In the meantime, though, you can be aware of potential pitfalls and do what you can to avoid them.

The Truth about Why You "Never Have Enough Time"

You *know* you should be doing more exercise and taking that evening walk you promised you'd take every day.

But you don't.

Why?

"I just don't have the time!"

Sound familiar?

Sure, it's a garden variety excuse, but it really does seem like every day, you run out of time, and every other thing eats up the available hours until there's nothing left to do those tasks you know you should do.

British historian Cyril Parkinson has an explanation for this phenomenon, and it's commonly written as:

➜   **Work expands so as to fill the time available for its completion.**

What does this mean? It means that if you wake up and you're a journalist with two articles to write that day, somehow you get them done by the deadline. If you only have half an article to write the whole week, somehow that's how long it ends up taking you.

Parkinson gave the example of an elderly woman who has literally nothing to do one day except write a postcard to her niece—something that objectively takes a few minutes to do. But by "Parkinson's law," she finds herself spending

- One whole hour selecting a postcard at the store
- A full 20 minutes planning to write something and lettering it out neatly
- Another 45 minutes to walk to the post office, maybe with a stop on the way to get coffee…

This one task can spread out and fill the entire day, so that if someone asked this elderly lady at the end of it to do them a favor, she may well say, *"I just don't have the time!"*

Fine, it's an extreme example, but the principle points to many things Parkinson criticized—for example, the fact that an organization would streamline and seemingly have less and less work over time, and yet administrative staff were as busy and numerous as ever.

A professor at the Science of Complex Systems at the Medical University of Vienna, Stefan Turner noticed the phenomenon in his university's medical faculty. After splitting from the main university, the newly independent faculty grew from 15 staff members to 100... even though the number of scientists stayed exactly the same.

The only thing that increased was the bureaucracy.

What happens with over-bureaucratization in big organizations can happen on an individual level, too. Without realizing it, you create "busy work" for yourself and start establishing hierarchies and task pyramids that, if you'd only look closely, serve very little purpose other than to make the task fit the available time (and, in some cases, eat up other available resources).

When Turner examined governmental cabinet sizes in different countries, he found that groups above 20 start to show lowered effectiveness, and emergent dynamics start to interact with one another rather than on solving the task at hand. On the personal level, this may look a little something like this:

> *You're writing a book that needs loads of research, and so you spend hours creating a filing and organization system to keep track of information. When this takes up too much time, you hire a PA, then spend too much time teaching them your system.*
>
> *They start making their own amendments to that system and introduce non-compatible apps and tools that you then have to upgrade to. You're both*

confused, so you plan a Zoom meeting, the first ten minutes of which is spent deciding what you'll talk about, and the last five deciding who will email written minutes to the other.

That evening, instead of sitting down to write the current chapter, you instead spend 20 minutes compiling an email to the PA asking for some missing information... After three weeks, you and the PA finally get a good rhythm going, but there's one thing that still hasn't happened: Not a word of the book has been written.

The above situation can go on almost indefinitely because of one thing, and **it's not a lack of discipline— it's too much time.**

Yes, TOO MUCH.

You can imagine one thing that would get both the writer and the PA to stop dawdling and get on with the book: a tight deadline!

If Parkinson's law is true, then we should be able to *contract* our tasks to fit the available time, too—within reasonable limits.

➜ **A deadline is a way to focus the mind and concentrate your attention.**

Yes, rushing and cutting corners can produce low-quality work, but we too seldom look at the drawbacks of the other extreme, which is that we can also lose effectiveness when *we take too long* to do something and lose our sense of urgency.

Here we uncover similar unconscious mindsets as we found when talking about the 10X rule or the 40% rule.

➜ If we perceive that we have plenty of time to complete a task, we may unconsciously slow down so that we finish at that time.

➜ If we expect a certain level of performance, we tend to deliver it—and that can go both ways.

TAKE ACTION: Write down three things in your journal that you believe you can't do right now because you "don't have the time." Be honest—is the real problem the fact that you simply haven't set yourself a deadline for these things? If so, choose one goal and give yourself a time limit to achieve it.

What can we do with Parkinson's law?

- First of all, if you have trouble with procrastination, **don't assume that getting an extension on a deadline will help you**—it may, in fact, have the opposite effect.

  o With a realistic but soon-ish deadline on the horizon, you are forced to focus on what really matters and to take action. Just like the ten-minute rule, if you only have ten minutes, you'd better make them count!

- What if you really do have a deadline that's far away in the future? Well, *artificially* **bring the deadline closer.**

  o Again, break down tasks into smaller chunks and set a non-optional deadline for each chunk.

  o Think in terms of days instead of weeks and months.

  o Ever find yourself pushing tasks off and saying things like, "Ah, well, it's only due in two weeks' time, so I won't worry about it"? That's a sign that your deadlines are poorly defined and your tasks are not sufficiently broken down.

The longer it takes you to get to a deadline, the more opportunities there are for distractions and diversions to catch you and make you procrastinate. The irony is that you waste time because you have so much of it, and then run out of it, anyway. Plus, you may assign yourself a whole world of extra busywork that never needed to be done in the first place.

There is also something called **"Parkinson's law of triviality," which states that people often give too much attention to trivial matters when trying to accomplish a goal.**

So the little old lady will waste time choosing just the right stamp for the postcard, and ruling lines in pencil on the postcard, then writing her message, then carefully erasing the pencil lines... all of it non-essential.

You're "busy," yes, and it's *technically* true that you "don't have any time," but it's not a question of lack of discipline—after all, you are working, right?

In a way, **you're being worse than lazy; you're being counterproductive,** loafing and dawdling under the guise of earnestly pursuing the goal you set for yourself.

If you recognize even a small part of yourself in the little old lady, take heart and realize that overcoming Parkinson's law is a wonderful thing because it will suddenly grant you "more time."

Here's how to avoid the trap:

Be Crystal Clear About Your Values, Your Vision, and Your Goal

If your boss one day asked you to move a series of mysterious boxes from one end of the room to the other, but said, "No rush, just get it done whenever you can," do you think you'd be doing that job with an ounce of motivation?

Would you *ever* get around to it?

It's impossible to finish a task with no clear endpoint. It's difficult to work if you have no clear idea of what you're really doing or why.

Clear goals need to speak to your values, but they also need to be specific and have a fixed deadline. Be very clear about exactly what needs to be done.

- By when
- How
- And most importantly, *why*

In a Team, Understand Everybody's Roles and Responsibilities

Don't assume.

If there's more than one player in the mix, you need to make sure everyone knows what they are doing and what they can expect others to do; otherwise, your energy will be spent trying to iron out miscommunications. Roles go beyond the simple task at hand; anytime people need to coordinate, there will need to be:

- **Drivers** – These people lead and corral others, keep time, and push people along.
- **Approvers** – Those who make final decisions (and spare you the limbo of indecisiveness).
- **Contributors** – They influence decisions by putting in their expertise and knowledge.
- **Informed** – Those who are simply kept abreast of what the decision ultimately is.

Even in a very simple collaborative project, outlining these roles will prevent dawdling, delaying, and buck-passing. People are more likely to be accountable if they and the group know what their role is.

Stay Focused

"Scope creep" = getting distracted by diversions that are *not* part of your goal.

Before you begin, **be clear about what's part of your project and what isn't**. Be firm.

Draw a fence around your priority and refuse to let other, less important things seep in and distract you. If you must, shelve things to take a look at later when the current project is done.

The Never-Ending Drama of Procrastination

The little old lady in Parkinson's example spent the whole day sending a single postcard. But if you're a chronic procrastinator, you might have admired her energy and dynamism!

If procrastination is really bad, you could instead have wasted the entire day playing word games on your phone, putting off writing the postcard until the post office closed and it was too late.

Procrastination is a serious problem and in many ways can be more stubborn and difficult to quit than the most firmly rooted addiction. If you suffer from procrastination, however, then you know one thing for sure:

➔ **You have a problem with self-regulation and something has gone wrong with your sense of self-discipline**.

There is no blame or shame in any of it, but it does warrant closer investigation.

Let's start with what we know about procrastination:

- First, people with this problem tend to try many, many times to get better and yet don't.
- They also tend to think in terms of "laziness" and poor character.
- And yet, no amount of beating themselves up or self-admonishment seems to make them do the work.

What does all this tell us? There are *reasons* you procrastinate, and if your solutions are not working, then that solution must have somehow missed the real reasons for your procrastination.

There's something else: **People don't procrastinate for the same reasons or in the same way.**

You may put off work because:

- You don't actually find the work important or interesting.
- The work feels too hard, intimidating, or even impossible.

- The work is too easy, and so you're too bored to do it.
- You find the work interesting and important... but distractions and diversions always seem to be a little *more* interesting and important.
- It's not exactly that you're avoiding the work, but that you lack a strong reason to actively do it.

And so on. The above reasons and the fact that procrastination looks a little different for each person make it *seem* like a complex problem. But it isn't.

➜ **Procrastination is simply a self-discipline failure, no more, no less**.

The excuses we make up to explain the problem of procrastination, and the many different forms of psychological and behavioral fallout, are all just *symptoms* of the same problem: lack of discipline and self-regulation.

> *Consider an alcoholic or a heroin addict. While it might be true that these people have compelling psychological aspects to their behavior, and while they have several reasonable-sounding justifications, and while there are no doubt cultural, familial, and even spiritual dimensions to their condition, the fact remains that there would be no problem if they were able to properly regulate both their inner experience and their external behavior.*

When you lack the ability to self-regulate (i.e., to consciously and willfully decide on your own state of mind and work to maintain a healthy and optimal balance), then you respond to life very differently from someone who has this ability. In the case of heroin or alcohol, it's easy to see what the temptation is: the pleasure of intoxication.

What about with procrastination?

When we procrastinate, we are likewise too sensitive to external cues of distraction and diversion. In a way, what we are addicted to is *any* fleeting environmental stimulus that promises a brief pop of pleasure. We delay the less pleasurable thing, our work, and instead let our attention chase after the fleeting pleasure.

Here, a fleeting "pleasure" doesn't have to be much to be perceived as more interesting than the work at hand.

- A notification on your phone
- A new browser window
- A fleeting idea crossing your mind
- Any little flutter on social media

For veteran procrastinators, almost *anything* is seemingly more interesting than the work they're meant to do, including doing nothing. They'll spend the morning mooching around their apartment, pottering in the kitchen, and thinking about whether to go for a walk or not... all of which are more pleasurable than just sitting down and getting on with the day's tasks.

A procrastinator may complain, "*Why* am I like this? Why can't I just do my work already?!"

The simple answer? **Because you prefer not to.**

- You are unwilling to delay gratification.
- You have let the impulsivity of your hindbrain take precedence over the logical and rationality of your prefrontal cortex.
- You have used up your willpower and are now finding it fatigued when you need it.
- You are not living by your values.

- You have planned poorly.
- But *mostly...* you don't do it because you prefer not to. That's it.

The task is difficult, it takes effort, and you would, understandably, prefer not to expend effort and instead relax. So you choose the immediate pleasure over the future pleasure.

→ Procrastination is not a failure to act—it is itself an act because it is a **choice** you make for the slightly more pleasurable activity in the moment.

It has become popular for people to suggest complex and colorful ways to trick yourself out of procrastination. You may be strenuously told, "You're not lazy; you just... " and then be told that the task does not match your expectations, or that the style of work doesn't match your natural temperament.

Perhaps the most common advice is: *Procrastination is a lack of motivation; therefore, to get the task done, you need to make yourself feel more motivated.*

This piece of advice will, in fact, do nothing to help cure your procrastination habit. **In fact, it might make it worse.**

If you believe that motivation is necessary for action, or even that motivation is the only condition under which you can work, then you are telling yourself the corollary that *it is impossible to do anything unless you're motivated.*

In other words? You can only do something if you like it.

Can you see the insanity of this unconscious belief?

It's insane because, with very few exceptions, the task you have to do will probably *not* be the most exciting thing on offer in any moment. Even a person in their dream job who is healthy, happy, and thrilled to be doing what they're doing will struggle to say that everything on their schedule is always more appealing than, say... not doing it.

Or watching Netflix.

Or taking a nap.

➔ **If you believe that motivation is necessary, then you put yourself in a passive position of *waiting*—waiting for inspiration or permission or some magical external force to come and push you into making the first step.**

You may use all sorts of tips and tricks to coax yourself into doing what you're supposed to be doing. Of course, these tricks *do* have value (the ten-minute rule, for example!), but they will never be more than quick fixes in the case of procrastination.

And when the quick fix fails, you are back at square one with your fear, laziness, or uncertainty.

In a way, *some of these tricks are in themselves a form of procrastination* since they put off the inevitable moment when we have to face up to our own desire for instant gratification... and choose not to fulfil that desire.

- Until we get real with ourselves
- Until we claim our own agency
- Until we act with self-discipline

... we are always at the mercy of the next fleeting desire—or the next productivity trick that promises reward without effort.

In reality, many tasks that we find objectively valuable and necessary are not enjoyable all of the time, or indeed, any of the time.

Many of these tasks take energy, effort, and attention. Many of them are difficult and sometimes unpleasant. *No matter what you do*, you are not going to enjoy every gym session or class or meeting or chore. But this doesn't mean that these things are not still valuable!

Action creates inspiration, not the other way around:

- You don't need motivation to start
- Just start, and your motivation will build as you carry on

Procrastination is a problem of poor self-regulation and discipline. But one big way to break out of this trap is to *stop assuming that there is a quick, easy way out.*

There isn't one.

You simply have to do your task (or even just begin it!) even though you are in the state of preferring not to. Because that's the power you have: you choose things not because they're momentarily pleasurable but because your rational and conscious mind has told you that they're the best choice.

From this perspective, **how pleasurable any particular temptation is is irrelevant**—you've decided what you want to do, and since you're the author of your life, that's what you do.

Self-regulation is:

- The power to act bravely *even though* you're afraid.
- The freedom to make the right choice *even though* it's not the comfortable choice.

- The satisfaction of taking intentional action *even though* it's not easy or pleasurable choice.

The next time you find yourself saying, "Ugh, I don't wanna," when it comes to a task you assigned yourself, stop and become aware of what's happening.

You don't *want* to do something?

That's fine!

Maybe you have good reason. **But it turns out your wanting is not required. Only your action is required.** You can go on feeling as unhappy about the task as you like... but do it nonetheless.

BE AWARE: Understanding this and applying it are two different things. The next time you find yourself making excuses, ask yourself, "Is what I'm doing moving me forward?"

If the answer is no, then take immediate action. Does analyzing all the philosophical and psychological reasons why you procrastinate actually move you forward? No? Then stop doing it.

The 70% Rule Is a Procrastination Buster

The 70% rule is a great trick to help you shift your mindset and help you act even when you're feeling uncertain, scared, or unwilling.

It's easy to remember:

→ **Agree with yourself that you WILL act when you're 70% sure instead of 100% sure.**

This rule was purportedly created by Jeff Bezos, who undoubtedly used it to help him achieve "escape velocity" out of a state of fear and indecision and get on the path of actually making choices, receiving feedback, and adjusting along the way.

What exactly are we "escaping"?

- Bigger life problems.
- An overall attitude of hesitation and avoidance.
- Unnecessary caution and fear around big decisions—including those that are important for our transformation and development.

Example: You want to pitch a book idea to an agent, but you're not sure. You don't feel 100% confident in the idea, so you pull back until you feel more ready.

You're stuck in fear, doubt, and hesitation. You're not at 100%. So you decide to wait until you are.

The 70% rule turns this around—instead, whenever you want to procrastinate, simply ask yourself, **"Am I 70% sure I want to do this?"** Variations include:

- "Am I 70% willing?"
- "I am scared, but am I 70% brave?"
- "Do I have 70% of what it takes to do this?"

If the answer is yes, then do it.

In other words, you're **lowering the threshold for taking action**.

You don't have to be 100% on board—but 70% is enough to get going!

Many procrastinators are secret perfectionists because they don't want to embark on a mission unless they're perfectly inspired, perfectly organized, and have a failproof, crystal-clear plan to get there seamlessly... after which everyone is waiting at the finish line, applauding. If they can't have all this, they don't even want to bother, right?

But **perfectionism of this kind can be nothing more than an excuse.** It mostly comes down to:

- Fear
- Not having faith in your abilities

If we judge the task as very difficult or unpleasant, *and* we lack faith in our abilities to rise to that challenge, then we may unconsciously push away the anxiety of it all by procrastinating.

That's bad for self-discipline.

Our minds might have told us two things:

1. The task is super, super difficult.
2. We are completely, utterly helpless in the face of this task.

But our minds could be wrong! This is where the 70% comes in and alters our perspective.

Let's say you use this rule—what does that look like?

Example:

> *Imagine you have to make a cold call to someone and ask for details about funding for an important project. You're terrified. You hate speaking to strangers on the phone, you feel like you're socially awkward at the best of times, and you're petrified it'll be an uncomfortable call that ends in embarrassing rejection for you. The worst thing is that you're not a pro at this and are worried they're going to discover you're missing information, have the wrong data, or have completed the forms wrong.*

Who wouldn't procrastinate on this task, right? Maybe you decide to do more "research" on the problem first and prepare a bit more...

But if you do procrastinate, you're drawing out the anxiety and excruciating anticipation. That "what if" feeling only makes you feel bad, and you're making it last as long as possible.

Instead, if you just act (even though you're scared), then you are in a new position: You get to see what happens and respond to *that* rather than your imagination's worst hypotheticals.

In other words, they could say yes, or they could say no, or perhaps they could say maybe in a few different ways. But either way, **you'll have new information on which to act.** You'll be on the path toward completing this goal rather than standing frightened at the start line, unable to get going.

Or, according to Bezos,

> "Most decisions should probably be made with somewhere around 70% of the information you wish you had. If you wait for 90%, in most cases, you're probably being slow. Plus, either way, you need to be good at quickly recognizing and correcting bad decisions. If you're good at course correcting, being wrong may be less costly than you think, whereas being slow is going to be expensive for sure."

If you're not 100% sure about the decision you're about to make, don't worry. **Few people ever are.**

➜ **When you act, you expose yourself to more information as you go.**

It's the same with fear—you may act when you only have 70% faith in yourself, but as you go, you grow more confident in your abilities. As we said in an earlier chapter, inspiration doesn't cause action, action causes inspiration.

It's a myth that we are only allowed to act when we are in a position of 100% certainty or fearlessness. If you make your phone call when you only feel 70% ready, a few possibilities emerge:

- The person on the phone says no and tells you why. It's disappointing, but now you know what to do next—fix the thing standing in the way.
- The person on the phone says yes, in which case—well done! You got the outcome you wanted without wasting too much time.
- The person on the phone gives some other, in-between answer. Let's say they ask you to wait for someone else to call you back. Again, it's disappointing, but at least you are getting somewhere.

Some people want to be invulnerable.

- They don't act unless they are absolutely sure that the outcome will be in their favor.
- They don't speak up unless they're 100% confident in what they're talking about
- They don't attempt something until they feel like they're already experts in it.

While this mentality might have worked in school, it doesn't translate so well in real life. That's because in many ways, we *learn by doing*. **If you're unsure, sometimes the only way to get surer is to act and see what happens.**

Let go of the idea of a black-and-white outcome. You can always start and adjust as you go—you are very seldom committed to one course of action that you cannot change. Starting a new job, relationship, or university course is a big decision to make, but nothing that cannot be reversed or tweaked after the fact.

Consider this:

- **Person A** is hemming and hawing about trying the new XYZ strategy with their business because they're worried about the risks. They hang back and don't take the leap, instead preferring to research and deliberate a little longer.
  - This research phase lasts a year.
- **Person B** has a similar business and is facing the same decision. They're not sure, either, but they're 70% sure. Within two weeks, they take the leap and try XYZ. The whole thing fails in a big way. It takes three months for the business to stabilize again. But this time, Person B knows what went wrong, and why. They try again, this time all the wiser. It's the XYZ strategy but with a twist.
  - In a year's time, Person B's business is making impressive strides.

And Person A? They've deliberated for a year and *finally* feel ready to take the plunge. They try the XYZ strategy (the one that Person B already knows doesn't work)...

At the two- or three-year mark, which company do you think will be in a better position? And who has a richer, more sophisticated understanding of their business, Person A or Person B?

As you can see, the irony is that when we are afraid of engaging with uncertainty, we actually prevent ourselves from gaining more knowledge because we shy away from the experience of trial and error.

We create the exact thing we think we're avoiding.

Action has costs, but so does procrastinating—and the thing it costs, *time*, is impossible to replace. Realize that **action is a risk, but it's also something else: a chance to test hypotheses, try things out, and learn something new.**

Let's take this all back to self-discipline and procrastination.

The Fear of Making Mistakes

Yes, we procrastinate because we're lazy and want instant gratification. But there could be additional reasons:

- We are unwilling to do it wrong
- We are afraid of starting down a course that we don't want to continue on
- We are focused on what others will think about it
- We are embarrassed about our inadequacies

Basically, we have told ourselves that any outcome other than complete success is intolerable. Its perfectionism. We don't want to be beginners awkwardly trying something new while others look on. We want to be in-control experts who act cool, calm, and confident. Except the experts got that way by being willing to look foolish every once in a while!

Tell yourself: **The potential reward of success is almost always greater than the potential cost of failing.**

We focus on:

- How bad it would be to fail.
- How embarrassing it would be to make a mistake.
- How disappointing it would be to take a wrong turn.

But what about what we *don't* focus on?

We don't see that when we make a mistake, we actually gain something:

- We learn how not to do it in the future.
- We gain experience.
- We gain confidence.
- We teach ourselves that we can try, fail, and continue on without the world ending.

These are lessons you never learn if you never take the leap and act.

You already know that your brain is programmed for procrastination, for erring on the side of caution, and for letting fear be in the driver's seat.

But you don't have to go along with that!

➔ **You can see your fear of failure for what it is, still feel that fear, and yet consciously choose that it won't be in control of you and that you will act anyway.**

You may learn that taking action is pretty freeing—*whatever the outcome.*

You get an enormous sense of courage from grabbing hold of your own autonomy and choosing for yourself. This is valuable, even if it doesn't pan out like you hoped. You still exercised your own free will, and that's a good feeling.

TAKE ACTION: Today, make a plan to deliberately fail at something. Seek out failure. It sounds counterintuitive, but challenge yourself. For example, ask out someone you know will say no, run the idea of a raise past your boss, or apply for a job you don't have much hope of getting.

Why? Well, try it yourself and see what happens.

Instead of:

- "I wonder what could go wrong?"

Genuinely become curious about the outcome, and ask:

- "If it does go wrong, so what?"
- "I wonder *why* it went wrong?"
- "I wonder what I can learn from it?"

One attitude is *passive* and *fearful*.

The other *curious*, *conscious*, and *self-directing*.

One attitude will keep you trapped in a prison of fear and doubt.

The other will accumulate and strengthen the more action you take.

There are many, many things in life that you don't *have to* do. Nobody is going to come and convince you to do things like upskill, look for a better job, leave a subpar relationship, or indeed, make any important life change.

Sadly, this makes it all the more tempting to put it off until tomorrow… i.e., never. **Think of your fear of "I'm not 100% ready yet" as a kind of trap that can only**

be broken one way: with forceful, deliberate, and courageous action.

Do You Suffer From "False Hope Syndrome"?

Picture this scenario: James set several lofty weight loss goals in the past, all of which have failed to ever materialize. But *this* time, James has hope.

This time will be different.

James has so much hope, in fact, that he has set multiple goals—many of them quite unrealistic...

Sound familiar?

Wanting to change is a beautiful thing. Feeling inspired and motivated to transform yourself is a powerful force—in fact, it has been with you all through life, encouraging your physical, emotional, and social development.

Psychologist Charles Richard Snyder created a "theory of hope," where he found that "high-hope" people tend to have improved ability to:

- Set a course to their goals
- Find alternatives when necessary
- Actually meet those goals

Hopeful optimism allows us to be *motivated, resilient,* and *focused.* So far, so good.

But hope isn't *always* useful. Sometimes, it can backfire and undermine our ability to reach goals.

False hope syndrome actually describes a process:

- **Step 1:** Hope leads to the creation of unrealistic goals.
- **Step 2:** We fail to meet those miscalculated goals.
- **Step 3:** We misunderstand the cause of our failure—the unrealistic goals—and instead blame ourselves, give up, or repeat the cycle over again.

So, let's say you decided you wanted to lose weight (a good idea), and you set yourself a goal (also a good idea). But the goal was to lose 40 pounds in one month (not a reasonable goal), and when you failed, you concluded that dieting never worked, that you had no self-discipline, or that you were doomed because deep down, you're just a bad person. Or all three!

None of these conclusions are true. None of them is the real reason you failed—you failed because you had *false hope* and set yourself a target you couldn't actually reach.

You may then decide to give up entirely... that is, until it's New Year's and you decide you're inspired again. This time, though, you're going to lose *50 pounds*. The cycle continues, and all that results is a feeling of failure and low self-belief.

You may have actually made some progress along the way—for example, losing ten pounds initially. This is a real achievement, but if you compare it against overly lofty goals, the only conclusion is disappointment.

We all sometimes miscalculate how much effort or time certain goals take:

- It takes more work than we guessed.
- It takes longer than we thought.
- The whole thing ends up looking a little different from what we predicted.

But the trick is to use hope to help us keep *adjusting* our goals rather than allowing overly inflated expectations to cause us to give up.

Research by Polivy and Herman found that inexperienced dieters tended to start out on a dieting mission with more initial excitement than veteran dieters... but also a greater chance of eventually giving up. Interestingly, even the veteran dieter participants who did succeed in losing weight still experienced a sense of failure and low mood.

This tells us something interesting:

➔ **Our *perception* of progress is important, and so are our expectations for what is possible for us.**

It may actually be better in the long run to guard against over-optimism and being too confident. These may be signs that you're emotionally attached to an impressive—but unattainable—goal.

Importantly, there's nothing wrong *per se* with failing or being disappointed by failure—rather, **what is damaging is misunderstanding the real cause of failure**. This means that having false hope is not a problem if you recognize it as such and make a correction:

> *"Oh, I guess that was asking for a little too much. Maybe losing ten pounds is actually good progress, and I should adjust my expectations a little."*

How do we know if our goals are based on unrealistic expectations? A goal is probably unattainable if it incorrectly estimates the:

- Ease
- Speed

- Quantity or
- Rewards

How do you know if you've incorrectly estimated? Well, you'll fail!

Example:

- **Ease**. You might set a weight loss goal and assume you'll reach it just by having brown rice for dinner instead of white. This is assuming the process will be easier than it realistically will.
- **Speed**. You might set a goal of losing ten pounds, which is totally feasible, but expect yourself to do it in an unrealistic time frame, like two days.
- **Quantity**. You might set yourself a reasonable weight loss goal but simultaneously try to start up a gym habit, change your sleep schedule, become a vegetarian, and quit drinking and smoking all at once.
- **Rewards**. You may do everything right and lose the weight you said you would in a comfortable time frame. And you *still* feel unhappy about your appearance and lack confidence. Why? You assumed the rewards of achieving your goal would be greater than they actually are. You haven't suddenly transformed into the perfect version of yourself, content with life forever more. You've just lost weight!

When you make a decision to change, you get a rewarding sense of being in control. Your motivation gets a boost—you feel powerful and on track, like you've suddenly seen the light. This can keep you going for a while.

But then something happens: Your initial burst of enthusiasm fades, and you're left with the plain and sometimes boring fact of the hard work you still have to do. Then what?

You have a choice:

1. Adjust yourself in whatever way you need to in order to keep going, OR
2. Throw in the towel, give up, and relapse.

As you progress toward a goal, the easy gains are won and improvement may slow or even stall. Adjusting your goals means getting real and understanding that *you haven't failed* **just because you are no longer super excited** about the goal or you've achieved something a little less than what you hoped for.

If you can hold off on feeling bad about yourself or the process, then you can start to ask genuinely useful questions, like:

- I'm stuck; what can I do to get moving again?
- What have I under- or over-estimated?
- What isn't working anymore?
- What *is* working?

This shifts your focus from negative **feelings** (which will only cause you to give up in shame or self-blame) and reorients you toward the only thing that will keep you on the course: consistent **action**.

➜ **We need to be able to stick with our goals even when they disappoint us by materializing in ways we didn't expect.**

The next time you are hit hard by a disappointing failure, notice the impulse to angrily throw in the towel, and ask three important questions first.

- Have you actually failed at all?
- If so, what is the real cause of your failure?

- What can you do to address that cause right now?

The first question reminds us that sometimes we perceive failure when we haven't failed at all—we are just progressing in a realistic way.

The second question reminds us not to automatically assume the worst and ascribe the failure to us, or to a universe that hates us.

The third question puts us back in a proactive frame of mind: Ultimately, what are you going to do about it?

***You* haven't failed, but your current strategy may not be working**.

Be glad for that useful bit of data.

Accept it as an invitation to learn to do better next time.

It may be strange to think about, but all the phenomena we've discussed in this chapter so far—allowing work to expand to fill the available time, procrastinating, holding off on big decisions through fear and uncertainty, and going on the boom-and-bust rollercoaster of false hope—all have something in common:

They are all forms of **avoidance**.

The biggest roadblock to developing effective discipline and self-mastery is allowing ourselves to avoid the challenge of hard work, of conscious choice, and of taking the difficult but more rewarding path. Even hope, when it is false hope, can be a form of avoiding the truth about how we create the life we actually want for ourselves.

BE AWARE: Take another look at some of the goals you wrote down for yourself in earlier chapters.

How realistic are they? Consider your failures in the past and ask what *really* caused them—the fact that you are incapable or the fact that your approach was flawed?

Chapter Takeaways:

- There are many self-discipline traps to avoid— for example, Parkinson's law, which states that work expands so as to fill the time available for its completion. Set yourself challenging but realistic deadlines. Instead, remember your higher goals, vision, and values, be clear about team roles, and stay focused to avoid "scope creep."
- Watch out for "Parkinson's law of triviality," which states that people often give too much attention to trivial matters when trying to accomplish a goal.
- Despite the ink spilled on the topic, procrastination is simply an issue of poor self-regulation and being too sensitive to external distractions and diversions. Be honest about why you procrastinate: Because you prefer to.
- To beat procrastination, don't wait for permission, inspiration, or motivation—just act. Action creates inspiration. Remember that your desire to do a task is not a prerequisite for doing it.
- The 70% rule is deciding that you WILL act when you're 70% sure instead of 100% sure. Sometimes the only way to get surer is to act and see what happens.
- False hope syndrome is when hope leads to the creation of unrealistic goals. When we fail to meet this miscalculated goal, we misunderstand the cause of our failure—the unrealistic goal—

and instead blame ourselves, give up, or repeat the cycle over again. Avoid this by asking, "What can I do to get moving again?"

Chapter 6: Making Good Friends With Discomfort

Your ancestors had a basic code for living: avoid pain; seek pleasure. And if something is scary, avoid that, too.

But as a conscious and self-determining human being, you know that there is some wiggle room for negotiation! In order to grow, you *must* feel some pain and fear sometimes.

The experience of growth is innately uncomfortable.

Nobody ever made sweeping life changes or achieved impressive goals without breaking a sweat or feeling a little flustered. It's hard. If it weren't hard, then *everyone* would be ultra-evolved and super successful, wouldn't they?

- Motivation is not necessary for action.
- Being 100% certain is not necessary.
- Feeling safe and comfortable is not necessary, either.

In this chapter, we'll look at how to ride out feelings of discomfort, temptation, and exhaustion so that we can reach our goals no matter what.

Yes, It's Uncomfortable. Embrace It!

People vary in their personal thresholds for pushing their limits and stepping outside of their comfort zones. Some people are more comfortable with being uncomfortable than others, but *anyone* can learn to test their limits and tolerate a little more adversity, uncertainty, or fear.

➜ **If you want to do something you haven't done before, by definition, it's not going to be easy and familiar to you.**

Remember the brain's preference for the status quo, and the cognitive bias that familiar things equal good things?

Reframe Your Fear

There is a big difference between being uncomfortable and being scared. And there's a big difference between how we respond to each emotion.

- **Uncomfortable** means you are doing something new and unfamiliar. You are no longer in your comfort zone, you cannot predict what will happen next, and you're not in perfect control. Maybe you're a beginner or doing something that feels a little risky or strange or vulnerable.

- **Scared** means we are aware that we're exposing ourselves to something that is genuinely dangerous or threatening.

Striking up a friendly conversation with someone you're attracted to may feel *uncomfortable*; going on a date with a convicted felon who's threatened you once is *scary*—and it should be!

Too often, however, people use words like "scary" to describe things in life that are *not* genuinely threatening or dangerous.

- Moving somewhere new
- Applying to medical school
- Speaking up when you don't agree with what's happening

These things are *uncomfortable*, yes, and they may be difficult or inconvenient or tricky. But this is not the same as the fear that alerts us to danger and keeps us safe.

The first thing to do when learning to embrace discomfort is to simply recognize it for what it is.

Discomfort.

That's all.

Not white-hot fear or anxiety or terror. Just discomfort. It's irritation rather than pain. It's not something out of the ordinary.

TAKE ACTION: In your journal, take ten minutes to quickly jot down all the things in life you're scared of—don't think about it too hard. When you're done, look at each item and ask if acting on that idea would be genuinely scary or just uncomfortable.

Separate out those fears that keep you safe... and those fears that just keep you comfortable. This latter list could be, with some courage, a road map to growth for you.

Self-discipline is having the courage to face your fears so that they can no longer limit you. How we talk about what scares us is important. The next time you're feeling negative about a possible change or hard work or a challenging situation, try altering your language to reflect *excitement and interest* rather than *fear*:

- "I'm not used to this."
- "This is different."
- "This isn't easy."
- "Woah, this is new!"
- "I'm still figuring it out."
- "This is a challenge for me."

If you describe problems this way, you bring them firmly back under your control and remind yourself that they're temporary. Whereas "I'm scared" keeps you where you are.

Deliberately Seek Out Discomfort

To be fearful is to be on the back foot. It's to be passive and wait for life to come to you, whereupon you only *respond* to it.

But if you have discipline, you can take charge and proactively choose your experiences yourself, take the first step, and seek out discomfort—on purpose. If you can do this, a few things happen:

- You stay in control.

- You prove to yourself it's possible.
- You break the momentum of fearful procrastination and avoidance.
- You learn something.
- You give yourself a burst of affirmation and reward—something to be proud of!

There are lots of ways to strategically invite discomfort into your life. It can be as minor as trying a new dish at a restaurant or saying "yes" to an invitation you'd ordinarily turn down.

As you do so, consciously tell yourself that the experience has value *even if you turn out not to like it.*

The payoff is not discovering something new but strengthening your willpower muscle and giving you a boost of confidence in the process.

- Is **fear of rejection** stopping you from connecting properly with other people?
- Your self-discipline challenge is to deliberately approach people where you fully expect to be rejected, thereby "inoculating" yourself against it.
- You cannot control what other people think of you, but you can control your own behavior and how you carry that rejection.
- Set yourself a goal for how many times you get rejected and see what happens.
- Is **social anxiety** is limiting your life?
- You can cultivate a strong sense of self-discipline by putting yourself into new social situations.
- If fear of being different is jeopardizing your goals, then take baby steps in being your authentic self, gradually putting yourself out there.

- Finally, one thing that "I'm scared" keeps us from experiencing is the joy of changing our mind or realizing that we've been mistaken in our beliefs and biases.
  - The **fear of being wrong** can be a particularly rich area in which to challenge yourself—seek out people who really disagree with you and hear their point of view without immediately responding.
  - Question your assumptions and don't be too quick to dismiss feedback from others.
  - Be more willing to say, "I don't know," or, "I made a mistake." It's more liberating than you can imagine!

TAKE ACTION: Write down five things that you have chosen not to do in the past because you were too afraid (or, truthfully, too uncomfortable). Rank them in order from least to most challenging, then push yourself to try to tick them off the list one by one.

If that seems too overwhelming, then break each one down into bite-sized chunks and tackle them that way.

Remember that everyone has a different threshold for risk and discomfort, so don't worry too much about what others are doing and simply focus on *your* unique comfort zone and how you can gently challenge yourself out of it.

Make an agreement with yourself today:

→ **Embarrassment, uncertainty, awkwardness, unfamiliarity, or discomfort are NOT necessarily signs that anything is wrong and that you need to stop what you're doing.**

The truth is that these feelings are also necessary for self-growth, and, in fact, moderate discomfort may be a sign that you're developing as a person—even if it doesn't feel like it at the time!

- Don't be too quick to decide if you like or dislike something.
- When trying out something new, give it a few tries before quitting, if you must.
- If you do feel discomfort, see what "positive spin" you can put on it (i.e., tell yourself it's a sign of progress, not a signal to stop).
- Finally, have a sense of humor about it and have a good laugh at yourself—in life, we are all beginners!

How to Become an Urge Surfer

One thing that is especially uncomfortable and which threatens our discipline is temptation.

Urge surfing lets you observe an urge without acting on it.

Dr. Alan Marlatt coined the term in the context of addiction recovery. Marlatt's technique compares urges to ocean waves, and the addict to a surfer navigating those waves.

The big idea? *Strong waves of temptation are powerful—but they pass rapidly.*

Remember that they won't last long, and give yourself the chance to surf that urge rather than being bowled over by it.

An urge is simply a feeling of intense desire for something.

That's all it is.

Importantly, it's *not* a compulsion to act.

You can intensely desire something natural and good for you (food, water) or something that has purely negative effects on you (cigarettes).

Does this mean just *ignoring* the distraction, urge, or temptation? Not quite.

This is because when you try to ignore something, you may actually end up giving it more psychological power and even prolong a sensation that would have ordinarily not lasted that long.

A concept or sensation usually becomes stronger when ignored, not weaker—after all, ignoring a wave in the ocean doesn't mean it's not there and you won't feel it crash into you.

So, how do you surf the waves of temptation rather than get knocked over by them? The answer is mindfulness. When we practice mindfulness meditation, what we are doing is teaching ourselves. We are learning to:

- Be fully in the moment without clinging to it or resisting it.
- Be *on top of* the wave rather than inside of it.
- To see and acknowledge our urges and feelings without identifying with them in any way.

If we can do this for long enough, the urge does pass and we are once again calm and balanced.

A Meditation to Help You Ride Out Urges

This meditation contains just two parts: First breathe, then notice. That's all.

Step 1: Breathe

First:

- Sit comfortably.
- Just slow down and relax for a second.
- Feel yourself "arriving" into the moment.

Now, the easiest way to get into the moment is to *breathe*.

Be in your body and your five senses, but start with your breath first—some deep and slow belly breaths (just like with "box breathing" we discussed earlier).

Step 2: Notice

It's just you and your awareness. What is your awareness aware of?

"Notice" means you *bring awareness to something,* but in this awareness there is:

- No judgment
- No interpretation
- No narrativizing
- No push or pull
- No fleeing to the past
- No projecting into the future

If you find your mind goes all over the place, gently call it back to the present by remembering your breath.

See if you can observe your urge from the outside in.

What does it feel like in your body?

What thoughts and emotions does it come with?

Maybe you're craving something you know you shouldn't eat. Do you notice a strange edginess or anxiety in the pit of your stomach? Just dwell on this feeling, exploring it.

Your mind may produce thoughts:

> *"Why bother meditating? Chocolate's good for you, anyway. It has antioxidants! What's the big deal? I don't know why you have to be such a buzzkill..."*

Just watch these thoughts coming and going like a wave. What does it feel like to **see these thoughts *as thoughts*** and not something you have to automatically start engaging with?

If you stay noticing for a while, you might see that the urge (with all its sensations, feelings, and thoughts) comes to a peak... and then subsides again, just like a wave.

Congratulations!

You've surfed that wave rather than drowned in it.

Most urges, cravings, and desires seldom last more than thirty minutes—even though at their peak, they can do a good job of convincing you that they are forever! Others may come. But they will pass just the same.

A few things to remember as you try this meditation for yourself the next time craving hits you:

- **There are two ways to "feed" an urge, temptation, or craving.**

- o   One obvious way is to give in to it.
- o   The other way is to try to violently avoid it, to force it away, to fight it, or to engage with it in judgment or shame.
- o   *Both* of these are like hitting the wave head on.
- o   It's only when you can stand back from a craving and let it be *without resistance or grasping* that you can "surf" it.
- **We can accept an urge without giving in to it**.
- o   It's there and that's fine. But giving in to it is a separate, unrelated choice.
- o   By urge surfing, you are showing yourself that there is an option you might not have considered—feeling the temptation fully but without succumbing to it.
- When the urge is *really* strong, i.e., at the crest of the wave, you can stay afloat by **holding on to your breath and your senses.**
- o   Just keep breathing and put your awareness onto your five senses.
- o   What are you experiencing? Don't give anything a label of good or bad, wanted or unwanted... just be curious about the moment's characteristics.

Here is an example of how the meditation might play out in the real world.

Daniel is not exactly "addicted" to social media, but it's a constant source of distraction, and he is trying to break the near-constant temptation to be checking his phone all the time. He finds that this habit breaks his concentration, gets in the way of socializing, and makes it easier to procrastinate.

Luckily, there are about four million opportunities for him to practice riding out the urge! He is sitting having dinner with his family, and his phone is on the table beside him. He could put the phone elsewhere, but what he really wants is to not simply avoid the temptation but learn once and for all to be master over it.

He realizes he's itching to reach over and check his phone. In this very instant, he stops and takes a few breaths.

This is the make-or-break moment, the margin in which his self-discipline is created.

He turns inward to notice what's going on with him.

A maddening desire to just check already!

He notices a fidgetiness in himself, and an impatience. As the sensation grows, he watches it crest to a peak that actually feels almost like anger. He settles in for the ride. He is not going to check his phone, but he is going to patiently wait and watch. With curiosity, he watches as a flurry of thoughts and emotions burst into his mind.

What if there's something important he's missing?

What if it's work?

What if...?

As he resists, this voice reaches screaming pitch until it's almost like a little child having a tantrum inside his head.

And all at once, it's over.

Within a few minutes, the sensations don't seem as strong. He sees himself sitting and riding it out, perfectly fine, without having checked the phone. Just ten minutes later, another wave comes. But this time, it's much less of a big deal.

"Oh, it's you again," Daniel thinks, and, for the first time, he finds himself genuinely more interested in the conversation around him and not his phone.

You might be wondering if it's worth doing the above meditation if you are experiencing "willpower fatigue." The answer is no. We all have fixed limits to our capacity to self-regulate, and we can exhaust these mental and physical resources.

→ The above technique is to be used *assuming everything else is as under control as it can be*. But it is obviously going to be much, much more difficult if you are tired, overwhelmed, ill, or trying to manage too many urges at once.

TAKE ACTION: You don't have to wait for external temptations to practice the above technique. Take control by exposing yourself to temptations, on purpose, to train your surfing skills. Consider it a form of meditation.

For example, arbitrarily decide to wait ten minutes before enjoying your dinner, just to see if you can. Be curious about the wave and what it will feel like. The stronger the temptation, the more you have to be grateful for—because it will teach you more. The next time you face external temptation, you're prepared and know what to expect.

Are You Undisciplined, or Are You Just Burned Out?

The outward signs of a lack of self-discipline may look very much like the signs of plain old burnout.

We've claimed that discomfort is not a reason to give up, but there is a caveat to this: Discomfort is not the same as burnout.

Burnout = a state of fatigue resulting from *prolonged* or *recurrent* stress.

Discomfort is a part of life and a part of growth, but too much discomfort for too long a period will have the opposite effect.

Most of us associate burnout with stressful careers and working too hard, but the definition is much broader than this. Any time we are experiencing a state of prolonged stress, whether that's

- emotional,
- mental,
- physical,
- psychological,
- spiritual, or
- social,

then we can be said to be burned out.

Discomfort can make us stronger

But ongoing *exhaustion* only depletes and weakens us.

Consider the example of Joely, who is a chronic procrastinator and feels like it's a mission to get herself to do anything at all, even the things she used to love most. She works as a teacher's aide in an underfunded and understaffed school in a bad part of town. Whenever she is asked how she is, Joely has one thing to say: "Tired."

Does she lack discipline? Is she just depressed?

No—depression and the lack of self-discipline are both symptoms of the bigger problem, which is that she's burned out. Joely's situation has a lot in common with other people who experience burnout:

- She has no control over how her job is done, but she is still responsible for when things go wrong.
- Nothing about her job resonates with her or her values.
- There are few rewards associated with doing well in her role.
- She has too many things to do, and usually does all of them, but poorly.
- She lacks support, feels isolated, and often has to do the difficult stuff on her own.
- The stakes are high, but sometimes she's not sure what she's supposed to do, and her priorities often conflict.
- Her supervisors are seldom around, and when they are, they micromanage. Their instructions are always unclear.
- She feels like a failure at what she does and lacks confidence in her abilities.
- The pay is low, the job isn't well respected, and Joely actually wonders if she'll even have the job in a few years' time.
- She used to care more and be excited about some aspects of her job, but this enthusiasm was never rewarded—and sometimes actually punished!

Some people have a similar situation, but instead of a career, it's a relationship that's wearing them down.

Just like Joely, they may feel too much responsibility and not enough control.

They may feel alone and trapped, lacking support, and as though nothing they do makes things better anyway.

You'll know that you're burned out when you feel exhausted, cynical, irritable, and even angry. But there's another big sign: **dread**.

Joely dreads going into school each day and is filled with a violently negative reaction every time someone asks her to do a task. When burnout is left untreated too long, it can lead to:

- Deep feelings of emptiness
- A lack of hope
- Depression

Basically, you feel like a car might feel when it's run out of fuel but still has to drive 100 miles!

Now, if Joely went to speak to a life coach who then diagnosed a lack of motivation and a poor sense of self-discipline, he might have suggested she *push through her discomfort*—which is exactly what got her into the problem in the first place.

Here's the question: **How do we know if we are undisciplined or if we are truly and genuinely burned out?** Firstly, let's look at the behaviors that both low-discipline and burnout share:

- Low productivity
- High distraction
- Disliking your job (even if your "job" is parenting, caring for someone ill, or managing a relationship!)
- Feeling rushed and overworked

But that's where the similarities end. Below are some tell-tale signs that you are experiencing burnout and not laziness or lack of self-discipline.

Red Flag 1: Mood Changes

If you're undisciplined, the strongest emotion you're likely to feel for an upcoming task is mild irritation. It's a little like that moment after a good lunch in the middle of a workday—it takes a push to get up and get on with work again, but that's all.

However, if the prospect of doing an upcoming task makes you feel...

- Genuine despair
- Rage
- Terror
- Debilitating fatigue

...then it may be burnout.

A big clue that you're burned out is that you keep feeling "tired" despite getting plenty of physical rest— a sign you are *emotionally* and *mentally* exhausted.

Red Flag 2: Physical Symptoms

- Stomach and digestion problems
- Headaches and migraines
- Chronic insomnia
- Aches and pains

These and a whole host of other "whack-a-mole" symptoms that seem to come and go all suggest burnout rather than lack of discipline.

The stomach is often the first place to show ongoing stress and anxiety (think ulcers and indigestion) but pay attention to your sleep and eating habits too (nightmares or changes in appetite).

Finally, consider it a serious problem *if you are using and abusing substances* in order to cope with a job or situation.

Red Flag 3: Anhedonia

Someone who is lazy and procrastinating may feel totally unmotivated to do a boring task... but that motivation pops right back when a more enjoyable task presents itself.

But if you're burned out, you may have difficulty summoning the energy or interest for even those things that you ordinarily relish. The word for this lack of ability to feel pleasure is called *anhedonia*, and it's a sure sign that you've been depleted for too long.

Red Flag 4: You Can't Think Straight

It's probably burnout if you find yourself having trouble concentrating, forgetting things, or can't find the right words. Your brain is an organ just like any other, and if it's overloaded, its performance starts to drop. Watch out for apathy, uncontrolled daydreaming, or feeling a bit "spacy" and disconnected.

<u>**Red Flag 5: You Are Hurting Others**</u>

If we have been exhausted for a long time, it's like we are in an energy deficit or debt. We can find it difficult to do *anything*, and that includes

- Being compassionate
- Having patience
- Being kind to others
- Having empathy
- Being able to listen

Those with poor self-discipline usually hurt only themselves, but if you find that your behavior is negatively affecting your relationships with other people, it's more likely to be burnout.

BE AWARE: Regarding the priorities and special tasks in your life right now, do you notice any of the above red flags?

If you discover that your problem is not in fact self-discipline but burnout, then your task is not to challenge yourself or embrace more discomfort—it's to **recharge**.

TAKE ACTION:

- See what you can do to gain more control over your work and make it personally meaningful and fulfilling to you.
- Reconnect with your values and reassess your current work situation—you might need to work less, make changes to your current style of work, or do completely different work.

- If work feels joyless, you may need to reintroduce more rewards and pleasure into the process.
- Avoid multitasking and focus on just one thing at a time.
- Ask for support, guidance, extra training... or seek out a mentor who can advise you.
- Set rock-solid boundaries and assert them when people demand too much of you.
- Try to remind yourself of your value and boost your confidence and self-faith by drawing on your past achievements.

There's no doubt that these things are challenging, and that many people do not have much scope to negotiate the terms of their work. But burnout is a sign that things aren't working, and one way or another, you will only continue on the path of exhaustion and low productivity.

Joely may realize, after working on her burnout problem for a few months, that none of the above suggestions work long term, and that bigger changes are in order.

Leaving a job can be a terrifying prospect—and completely changing careers even more so. But if you make the leap toward something that fits you better, you may find that the necessary energy and enthusiasm you need will be there in abundance!

The Best Way to Deal With Burnout

The best way to deal with burnout is to avoid it in the first place.

Discomfort and temptation can be "surfed," but burnout is very difficult to reverse once it's underway.

As you develop your self-mastery, it's wise to develop a set of corresponding habits:

- Knowing when to pull back
- Knowing when to rest and recuperate
- Knowing how to strategically use self-care to manage your resources

Focus on Self-Efficacy

In Joely's case, not having any real say at work significantly undermined her ability to care about what she was doing. Her role lacked **self-efficacy, which is a person's belief in their ability to behave in ways that get them what they want.**

Every human being has these needs. We all want to feel:

- That we matter as people.
- That our actions and intentions make sense.
- That it's possible to make a difference.
- That we know what the "rules of the game" are when it comes to achieving our goals.
- That we are capable of learning those rules and playing by them.

Without any of this, *without self-efficacy*, our tasks can feel pointless, unfair, confusing, or unjust.

This is why **the difficulty and complexity of a job or task is *not* a predictor of whether you'll burn out doing it or not.** If you are attempting really challenging tasks, but you feel that you are able to make headway and find real progress with it, the task will feel inspiring and encouraging.

Similarly, even if a task is relatively simple and straightforward, if you doubt your own self-efficacy when doing it, you risk burning out.

You'll know you need a greater feeling of self-efficacy if you struggle feeling confident in your work and don't have a clear answer to the question, "What's next for me?"

Self-efficacy is something that comes from a particular job or role (or even the way you're led and managed), but there's a lot you can do to increase your self-efficacy on your own terms.

TAKE ACTION:

1. **Don't wait for others to assign you milestones**—set yourself small goals and give yourself a reward when you achieve them.
2. **Identify a role model** for yourself and see what you can learn and apply from their lives into your own.
3. **Be authentic about your goals.** Goals alone won't motivate people or give them meaning—they have to be goals that genuinely speak to values. Take the time to figure out why you're really doing something and set appropriate goals. If this feels impossible to do in your current job, it's probably time to move on.
4. **Don't sell yourself short.** Get out of the habit of downplaying your achievements and be proud of the gifts you have.
5. **Keep learning.** Nothing will make you feel more in charge of your own trajectory than

deliberately choosing to expand your knowledge and learn a new skill.

Focus on Needs, Not Tasks

When there's a poor job–person fit or your current role isn't working for you, it's tempting to look at yourself and see all the things that don't quite match. You might also focus on the tasks you have to do rather than the motivation and meaning behind those tasks.

Get a fresh perspective by reminding yourself of what you need, as well as the fact that you are entitled to seek out work that suits your temperament and serves these needs.

TAKE ACTION: What are your needs? Take the time to outline them for yourself; here are some common ones:

1. Being authentically yourself and having integrity.
2. Feeling that your work has meaning and purpose.
3. Feeling "in the loop" and properly communicated with.
4. Knowing that what you do makes a difference.
5. Not having to follow pointless rules!

Once you are crystal clear about what you need not just for a particular task or in a particular workplace but with work in general, then you can work to meet those needs yourself.

Focus on Self-Care

If you do not proactively choose to prioritize your relaxation, balance, and well-being, it's unlikely that someone will come along and sort it out for you on your behalf!

- Sometimes burnout happens because people get caught in a cycle of over-extending themselves.
- This causes everyone around them to expect more from them.
- When the pressure is on, these people overextend themselves even further, and the cycle continues.

A little preventative self-care, though, would have stopped the cycle long before it got out of hand.

Self-care means self-regulation.

- Take breaks when your tank is nearing empty.
- Put up a boundary to protect yourself when necessary.
- Say no to demands you know you can't meet.

If you have a busy and draining life, it is also your responsibility to find things that fill you up again. One important part of self-care is realizing that you cannot do everything yourself and that it is an act of mature self-discipline to seek out the help of others, to delegate, or to ask for honest advice and feedback.

Switch Tasks
In Joely's case, drastic measures were needed, and for many people, the answer to burnout is indeed quitting

their jobs or changing their careers. On the other hand, for many people, it's a simpler problem to solve, and the answer is *better organization*.

Burnout can be avoided and treated by adding more careful structure to your day and paying conscious attention to *how* you work, not necessarily *how much* you work.

A big part of this is being mindful of how you switch from one activity to another—for example, how you end your professional time and begin your personal time.

The major shift to remote work brought by the Covid-19 pandemic has made people far more aware of the need for a kind of "organizational hygiene."

TAKE ACTION:

- Try to have the main portion of your workday structured and predictable. Block off periods in your schedule where you work and only work.
- Don't multitask. If you're relaxing with family, do that without letting work worries encroach. If you're at work, make sure your family knows you're unavailable.
- Have enough discipline to start each day with a productive task that makes you feel proud and grounded. This could be as simple as making your bed or doing some exercise.
- If you work at home, set up a distinct work zone rather than letting tasks overlap and bleed into one another. Set timers, and when you're done,

physically get up from your space to signal to your mind that you have changed your focus.

- Have some ground rules when it comes to screens and work correspondence. For example, decide you will not check your email after a certain point in the evening, or that you won't keep stressful and distracting devices on your bedside table.

- Schedule breaks, but don't go solely on time to judge when you need to pause and recuperate. Pay attention to your emotional and physical state, too, and take a break *before* you feel depleted.

Chapter Takeaways:

- The experience of growth is innately uncomfortable, so we need to get used to it! Understand that fear and discomfort are not the same thing, and deliberately seek out discomfort on your own terms to inoculate yourself against it. Remember that embarrassment, uncertainty, awkwardness, unfamiliarity, or discomfort are not necessarily signs that anything is wrong or that you need to stop what you're doing.

- "Urge surfing" is about riding the waves of temptation instead of succumbing to them. Try a two-step meditation where you 1) breathe and 2) notice urges without responding to them. Don't feed an urge by either giving in or fighting against it—just observe and accept.

- Discomfort is a part of life and a part of growth, but too much discomfort for too long will only cause burnout. Look for the red flags to suggest that it's time to replenish, not push through: mood changes, physical symptoms, anhedonia, cognitive impairment, and negative effects on other people.

- The best way to deal with burnout is to avoid it in the first place. Do this by increasing self-efficacy (a person's belief in their ability to behave in ways that get them what they want), think about needs instead of tasks, prioritize self-care and rest, practice "organizational hygiene," and keep things varied by switching tasks.

For those wanting to develop not just a superficial sense of self-control but a deeper feeling of mastery over one's entire experience through awareness, Zen Buddhism might hold some valuable insights. With its roots in Chinese philosophy, Zen is a blend of Mahayana Buddhism and Taoism and has now successfully spread to the West.

Zen is a way of encountering reality.

For practitioners of Zen Buddhism, it is possible to access the nature of reality and the nature of self *directly*.

- No theory
- No symbols
- No language
- Not even the application of reason and logic

It is a deeply mystical path that often (deliberately) appears paradoxical.

The awkward conclusion, then, is that Zen is not really something you can write about or read about—it is only something you can *experience*, and there is only one place you can experience it: right now.

"Enlightenment" is not, according to Zen, a question of arduous effort or of intelligent understanding, but of spontaneous realization. To reach this realization is not a question of intellectual study or logic. Instead, the path is meditation—an activity the mind may be very unfamiliar with.

Zen's non-dualistic, non-intellectual, and non-rational spiritual practice could help immensely with self-discipline since the approach is about cultivating conscious awareness—the bedrock for any deliberate and self-directed action.

To access the insights of Zen, we meditate. During meditation:

- We are encountering what is, without grasping or avoidance, without identification, and without ego.
- We see that there is something that exists before our thinking minds.
- We do not dwell on mental pictures and symbols and ideas about the past or the future; we are alive only to what is real, which is the continuously unfolding present.
- We are aware of duality, interpretation, and ego. But these things come and go like ripples on the surface of reality—which is unchanging, and of which we are a part.

"Zen" is, in fact, a Japanese word for meditation.

- The path of Zen.
- The idea of Zen.

- The action of Zen.
→ They are all one and the same.

Zen is something you *do* and something you *are*.

The original founder and teacher of Zen, the Bodhidharma, taught that the nature of reality could be learned outside of scriptures, letters, and words and could be discovered within yourself, in your own mind and in your own awareness. In fact, to do so would allow us all to become Buddhas (or rather, to realize that we all have Buddha nature already).

To meditate, then, is not to do anything special in particular except be aware.

Like many other forms of meditation, there is a focus on the breath and a calm and soft attention to what is unfolding in the moment. And, like other forms of meditation, new practitioners may find the process boring, uncomfortable, confusing, or strange.

→ **Meditation builds discipline, but it also requires discipline.**
→ **Focused mindful awareness is both the result of self-discipline as well as its cause.**

In a way, practicing meditation is like getting to the very heart of the self-discipline problem. Many people describe how the insights gained on the meditation cushion have been translated to every area of life.

This makes sense; no matter what our challenges are (emotional, behavioral, cognitive), at some point, we perceive them fundamentally on the level of awareness. If we learn to master ourselves on this basic level, we are much better equipped to regulate ourselves in anything that we do.

How to Do Zazen

Zazen is sitting meditation.

It is Zen in practice.

The first thing to know is that **sitting practice is goal-less and practiced without judgment**. This alone is a major roadblock, and experiencing what this means is a big part of the Zen practice.

- The goal is not to become a Buddha or be enlightened.
- The goal is not to become a really, really good practitioner.
- There is no goal at all—you just sit.

This may fly in the face of everything that you've ever believed about discipline and self-control, i.e., that it is a constant *effort* to continuously judge your experience, shape it, interpret it, and have an internal opinion about it.

But really, one of the most difficult lessons to master in Zen is to relinquish this striving, grasping, and identification.

You are not even "trying" to be goal-less. You are just sitting.

To do a sitting practice, you have to sit, naturally.

- Assume a posture that is upright, alert, and attentive.
- The idea is that your back is straight and erect, while your front is soft, yielding, and receptive ("hard back, soft front").
- There are a few positions to try, and variations include placing one ankle in front of the other,

sitting upright in a chair with both feet flat on the ground, or even kneeling and using your own heels as a kind of cushion.

- Hands can be placed gently on the lap, relaxed and open, or held against the lower belly, with the fingers clasped and the thumbs pressing against one another. This gentle pressure can become like a point of contact to the present moment, and you can ground yourself in this sense of touch.
- In Zazen, the eyes are typically kept open and softly gazing at nothing in particular.

Now, the breath.

Your breath is there and you are aware of it, but you are not trying to control it or force it to do anything either way. *Feel* it rather than watch it obsessively. Once you settle into a position and begin sitting and breathing, you will instantly notice that your mind wants to do everything it can to escape that moment!

- Your thoughts may wander to upcoming chores or events.
- You might think, "I'm bored" or "Am I doing this right?"
- There may be momentary flutters of emotion as you remember things that have happened in the past or anticipating things that are coming in the future.
- You may hear sounds outside that you immediately judge as negative or positive.

But just *notice* all this.

Notice that your thoughts are jumping all over the place, and you are just sitting. Your thumbs are still pressing together, and your breath is still going in and out, just where you left it.

You are sitting.

Your mind will throw up all sorts of interesting diversions and perceptions...

- "Zen is stupid. It doesn't even make any sense!"
- "You're a loser."
- "Seriously, I'm really, really bored."

But again, as you are aware of all this happening, you just watch it all go by. Your awareness comes back to the breath, back to the present, and, eventually, the thoughts evaporate again.

What were they, anyway?

Nothing.

As transient and insubstantial as clouds in a blue sky.

There is no need to judge the process or yourself. You are not getting a report card at the end of it, and there are no prizes and no judges to award them.

It doesn't matter if your mind wanders five million times during a meditation session. Watch it go five million times, and watch it come back five million and one times.

Sit still.

Just be.

That's all.

A Meditation Habit

Meditation will provide the most benefits when done *consistently.*

It may seem at times like a big chore to push through, or you may feel discouraged because you wonder whether you are getting anything from the practice or progressing fast enough. But it's precisely at this point that you stand to gain the most, because it's *here* where you strengthen your discipline.

You need to see distracted, bored, or judgmental thoughts emerge, and be patient and diligent enough to watch them pass again. Think of meditation as the continual brave encounter with the present moment, even when your mind wants to rush everywhere but the present moment.

The more you practice, the easier it becomes.

- At first, challenge yourself daily to complete just ten or twenty minutes at a time.
- Choose the same time every day, when you know you won't be disturbed.
- Gradually work your way up to longer sessions.
- If you feel ready, you may even seek out the support of a teacher or join a class where you can meditate together—the sense of shared accountability will help you keep turning up to the meditation cushion, even when you don't feel like it.

If you're facing strong resistance, be grateful—this, too, is just a part of your practice. Like you did with urge surfing, **don't feed the impulse by clinging or resisting**.

Perhaps you suddenly realize your mind has been wandering for the last five minutes.

➜   Fine. Notice it and come back to your breath without judgment.

Perhaps you *do* feel judgment and think, "I'm doing this wrong." What then?

➜   Notice it and come back to your breath without judgment.

Perhaps you do come back to your breath and think, "Nice! I'm getting better at this."

➜   Notice *that*, too, and come back to your breath without judgment.

Soon, you see that no matter where your mind goes and what your emotions do... you literally *cannot* escape the present moment.

Zen Meditation Master Dogen said,

> "To study the Buddha Way is to study the self, to study the self is to forget the self, and to forget the self is to be enlightened by the ten thousand things."

As we meditate, we realize that we are one and the same with all reality, and we see into the nature of this reality. We see perceptions, feelings, and thoughts emerging and falling away again, like a dance or music. After a while, even our awareness no longer seems to be there—only reality is, quiet and still yet somehow moving all the time.

You are relaxed yet perfectly alert.

You simply are, without push and pull, without struggle or effort.

Think of reality like a deep pool of water:

- When we are tangled up in countless thoughts and feelings, it's like the water is disturbed in waves and ripples.
- But if we let these dissipate, the surface of the water becomes smooth and flat—and reflective. We can suddenly see into the depths and maybe see ourselves reflected back.

When we lack discipline, we are unable to voluntarily choose to come to this natural and innate stillness. Our minds and perceptions are constantly flitting around, never resting anywhere, being blown around this way and that way.

Zazen practice reminds us of a deep truth: **We are aware and can choose whether to engage in these momentary distractions or not**. We can choose the calm fullness or to run after a tempting thought and let it carry us somewhere unawares.

We can choose discipline.

We can choose mindlessness.

Again, Zen meditation is not something to read about, but something to do. Try to see what it really *feels* like to let go of narratives, of ego, of grasping and resistance, and instead, just encounter head-on that vibrant, complete, and totally relaxed living moment that you are always inside of.

If you find yourself in mental knots or feeling chaotic and distracted, embed yourself down into your senses:

- Rub your fingertips against one another so that you can literally feel the ridges of each fingerprint.

- Feel the weight of the air as it flows in and out of your nostrils. Can you discern a difference in temperature between the inhale and exhale?
- Listen to what the silence sounds like around you. Feel it against your skin.

If you can dwell in these sensations and simply be with them, you'll also give yourself the chance to notice something: Life ticks along perfectly without your constant mental chatter!

TAKE ACTION: Right now, schedule your next (or maybe first) meditation session. You decide how long you want to go for, but once you've decided, do it no matter what. Agree with yourself ahead of time that there will be no judgment—not even of your own tendency to judge!

The Meaning of Shikantaza

Zen's "simply sitting" practice is also called shikantaza, or "just being."

Unlike most forms of meditation (and the form we explored in the previous section), shikantaza is completely object-less, meaning we don't focus on an object (such as the breath, mantra, or sensations) at all.

It is "non-thinking."

- You don't need permission or training.
- You don't need to follow any particular school or philosophy of Buddhism or Zen.
- You don't need to delve too deeply into the religious traditions.

You just *be*.

In fact, you've probably already done shikantaza before without realizing it. Maybe you've been outside in nature, alone and quiet, and simply noticing the view. It's hard to explain the fullness and simplicity of these moments. Your mind empties, and you are just there, being.

The troubles and distractions of the world were all still there, but you are somehow apart from that, and it didn't quite matter.

- This is a state of mind that you can access anywhere, at any time.
- You don't need a cushion or any particular body posture or hand pose.
- You don't need to block out "meditation, twenty minutes" in your schedule and set your alarm.
- Everything you need you already have—your awareness and the present moment.

Here are some examples:

- Pause after washing the dishes to watch the way the pillowcases are gently swaying on the laundry line outside.
- Before you go to sleep at night, lay in bed with just yourself and the moment, feeling the world quietly move around you just so.
- In the bath, get a little lost in the way the blue-gray line of the surface of the water swells and falls back as you move your knees underneath it.

In time, your mind will flash awake again with a million thoughts and images and worries and distractions. But enjoy the quiet, empty spaces that open up when you can let that mental traffic go for a moment.

It can be supremely refreshing, peaceful, and comforting to let the moment be as it is—**sufficient, without struggle, effort, or force.** Eventually, even the pillowcases on the washing line disappear, the bed disappears, the blue-gray line of water disappears, and so do you.

All that's left is being.

Meditation is a great practice to include in your life, but that doesn't mean you can't practice shikantaza whenever you remember: On the bus home, in the bathroom, or standing in the queue at the grocery store. This is because, while formal meditation practice has enormous benefits for self-discipline, there is nothing special about sitting here or sitting there.

The present moment is everywhere, and we always have access to it.

TAKE ACTION: In the art of just being, mother nature is the ultimate expert. Find your nearest snoozy cat and notice their behavior. Watch crows. Sit underneath a tree for a moment and try to emulate its stillness and calmness.

Rest your eyes on ocean waves that come and go, or listen to grass rustling in the wind. Being immersed in the natural world is a quick and surefire way to embrace the fullness of the present. Try to be in nature every opportunity you get.

What about today?

Think Like a Shaolin Monk

Zen Buddhism can bring extra depth and dimension to our everyday attempts to develop greater self-discipline.

It is one thing to master our environment and to be bigger than temptations and distractions.

But it is another thing to master *ourselves*.

If we can master ourselves, then we are strengthened in the face of *any* adversity, discomfort, problem, fear, or temptation. Some would say that there really is only one adversary in life, and that is the self.

A navy seal, boxer, or elite athlete will approach self-discipline in one way:

- They'll dominate their fears
- They'll push through pain and discomfort
- They'll try to develop mental toughness

A Shaolin monk will do the *same thing*, but in a different way.

From the perspective of the ancient Shaolin culture, **finding meaning and purpose in life is the only real goal, and finding our path to that in a world filled with illusion is the real challenge.** Therefore, mastery is not ultimately about earning a lot of money, becoming powerful, or getting six-pack abs.

It's about removing the obstacles in the path toward real truth.

Temptations, distractions, and intimidating challenges are like a fog that makes us lose sight of what's important and who we really are. Yes, we need to master our base urges to eat junk food or watch garbage on the TV, but the *reason* we do so is because these things are in our way on the path to self-discovery.

Without knowing that you are on this bigger, more important journey, the junk food and TV will distract and trap you.

- Your goal is not to have *self-discipline.*
- Self-discipline is just something you need to help you achieve your real goal: *self-discovery.*

The Shaolin approach posits **five hindrances on the journey to self-discovery.** These are not specific behaviors, thoughts, feelings, or choices, but **states of mind** that give rise to all these things.

Hindrance 1: Sensual Desire

Basically, temptations that stimulate your five senses. Follow these and you are at their mercy instead of following the path to deeper truth.

How much of your day is controlled by:

- Addictive junk foods
- Caffeine
- Pornography
- Easy consumerism
- Alcohol, cigarettes, or other substances
- Even just the temptation of your supremely comfy sofa?

Hindrance 2: Aversion and Ill Will

Negative emotions can pull us off the path.

A strong negative emotion may have nothing to do with the five senses but nevertheless have a strong hold on us and prevent us from claiming our own agency, willpower, and choice.

- Emotions are a part of life.
- *Negative* emotions cannot be avoided or ignored.
- But as we've seen, if we don't *process* them, *master* them, and *let them go*, then they will distract and confuse us.

Have you been distracted from a higher goal by emotions like fear, regret, resentment, or guilt? You may never have considered it before, but addiction to negative states of mind can be as life-limiting as an addiction to heroin or gambling.

Hindrance 3: Heaviness and Dullness

What Shaolin cultures classify as apathy, depression, and a lack of motivation. In the Buddhist framework, depression is not so much a mental illness or disease but a state of mind that is like imprisonment.

Hindrance 4: Restlessness

The path is long. It requires sustained attention in one direction to travel it. "Restlessness" = diversion, distraction, and scattered mental energies.

If you are confused about your priorities, lack purpose, or feel like you're juggling a million things at once, you are not traveling the path so much as running around in frenzied circles! The Buddhists call this illusory busy-ness "monkey mind," and it's a big, big reason for many of us stalling on the path.

Hindrance 5: Doubt and Skepticism

This is like a built-in anti-cheerleader who works to undermine, jeopardize, and second guess everything in your life.

- A lack of faith...
- A lack of trust...
- A lack of self-belief...

These things can make you believe the lies your own mind tells you and keep you from moving along on the path to self-discovery. If you are indecisive, cynical, or unable to believe in yourself and your dreams, you've allowed this particular hindrance to get in your way.

In a way, you become your own obstacle.

From the Shaolin perspective, self-discipline problems are a mix of all the above, particularly heaviness/dullness and restlessness.

How do we get around these obstacles?
How do we get back on the path?
Luckily, there's a four-step process.

TAKE ACTION:

- **Step 1: Recognize** what is happening.
- What is your state of mind?

o   See your thoughts as thoughts, your feelings as feelings.

- **Step 2: Accept** that this state of mind is your reality right now.
o   Acknowledge that it's there, without judgment.

- **Step 3: Observe** and investigate what came before this mental state.
o   How does it affect you to think and feel this way?
o   What are the costs and consequences?

- **Step 4: Gain distance** from this state of mind.
o   You are not your mind.
o   You are not your thoughts.
o   You are not your emotions.

Let's see how this might play out in real life.

Step 1: You're feeling stressed out and procrastinating on your day's tasks. You **recognize** your frame of mind:

- Avoidant
- Negative
- Restless

You identify a whole range of thoughts and feelings, from a sense of despair at your own abilities to a desperate urge to flee the discomfort of that feeling with escapist TV.

Step 2: When you notice this feeling, though, you stop short of judging or assessing it. You don't get carried away with shame and frustration (after all, these negative feelings are just another hindrance, right?).

You just imagine your state of mind set out in front of you on a table, and you look at it and **accept** that it is what is currently true for you right now.

Step 3: You **observe** and investigate a little further.

- You can see that the fear of performing badly and being judged is causing you to procrastinate.
- You can see that this in turn is creating more stress and undermining your efforts.
- You see that your mindset is not working—i.e., you realize that thinking this way is genuinely a hindrance and stopping you from doing what you really want to do.

Step 4: In your mind's eye, you imagine yourself picking up each item on this mental table and deciding if you want to hold on to it anymore.

- Is it helping to feel inferior and doubtful of your own abilities? No? Then set that aside.
- Only carry with you the things that don't get in the way.

In this visualization, you **gain psychological distance** from this mindset. That way of thinking and being is not who you *are*; it is just something you're currently choosing to *do*. Do you want to continue choosing it?

And that's it.

You don't have to feel ashamed or disappointed about where you are (another obstacle) or get trapped in trying to run away from or deny the obstacle (non-acceptance is—you guessed it—just one more hindrance on the path).

You just need to realize that with awareness, your state of mind, any state of mind, becomes optional. You always have the power to ask:

- *Is this really serving me?*
- *Is this helping me along on my way?*

The above technique may seem simple, but it's not easy, and mental training like this is what has made Shaolin monks famous all over the world for their discipline.

Mental and spiritual strength takes consistent training just as bodily strength does. Though Shaolin monks practice Kung Fu, their higher vocation is essentially to be a *warrior of the mind* and to battle the inner diversions that keep them from their true path.

Self-control brings *balance*, *calm*, and *integrity*.

The eight-fold Buddhist path of the Shaolin monk means cultivating

- Right intent
- Right understanding
- Right speech
- Right livelihood
- Right concentration
- Right mindfulness
- Right effort
- Right action

So, let's return to the conundrum we began this book with: It's lunchtime and you're faced with a choice:

- A nice healthy salad
- A diet-destroying cheeseburger and fries

At first, making the right choice is something that happens on a superficial level only. But with practice, you can start to think like a Shaolin monk: **The correct choice is the one that aligns with your higher, truer purpose,** and what doesn't align in this way is willfully ignored.

Because while your neurotransmitters, hormonal responses, and conditioned habits play heavily into the choice you make, ultimately it's *the strength of your will and your spirit* that is the most powerful.

- A Shaolin monk can stand outside of his body's sensual desires.
- He can stand outside his fear and his laziness.
- He can stand outside the flutter of thoughts that bombard him in every moment.

To approach the problem on this level is to play the game on a completely different playing field. If you were simply on a "diet" and felt that you'd better force yourself not to have the burger and fries you really wanted, you are not much more than an animal who has temporarily muzzled themselves.

But if you realize that **responsibility and discipline are a form of freedom**, you empower yourself to completely change your mindset.

As St. Augustine said, "Man has as many masters as he has vices." When you face the choice of what to have for lunch, you are really being tasked with choosing between:

- Having your desires, fears, and weaknesses be your master, or
- Having no master, but being consciously and willfully driven to pursue what really matters.

When you frame it like this, what temptation could possibly seem worth it? What distraction or addiction could compete?

Using Meditation to Build Self-Discipline

- Jack Dorsey leads Square, Inc. and Twitter, Inc. while attending congressional hearings and serving on Disney's board.
- Mark Wahlberg is an Oscar-nominated actor, owns many businesses, and takes his kids to school.
- Dwayne "The Rock" Johnson went from college football player to pro wrestler to actor. He wakes at 3:30 a.m., works out six days a week, and makes three movies and a TV show annually.

What do they all have in common? Self-discipline.

How do these three men build that self-discipline? Through meditation.

Each of them starts their day with morning meditation to help them focus, prioritize, and process their thoughts.

- **Meditation** allows us to be in the present and aware of our thoughts, emotions, and perceptions.
- From that present moment, **self-discipline** allows us to make the best decision for ourselves and take action no matter what our thoughts, perceptions, or emotions are.

Meditation helps us concentrate our minds, find balance, refresh our motivation, and face whatever comes our way with resilience and equanimity.

➜ When we are mindful, we are in charge of ourselves and can choose.

And the best way to develop this mindfulness is through meditation, which sets us *outside* our automatic habits, our fears, and our irrational cognitive traps.

Meditation doesn't make us superhuman, but what it can do is open up a brief window of awareness; in that window, we can remind ourselves to be better and to do better.

We can grasp the choice:

- Do we want our lower selves to control and dominate us?
- Or do we want to be guided, strengthened, and inspired from our innate wisdom and reason, instead?

Think of any successful or happy person and you will see that you possess precisely the same access to awareness, balance, and self-determination as they do. That's a powerful realization: *you already have the tools you need to be successful; it is only up to you to grasp those tools and learn to use them every single day.*

- Mark Wahlberg explains how he starts his day with prayer, gratitude, and a focus on his responsibilities for the day.
- Dwayne "The Rock" Johnson talks about two hours in the early morning where he just quiets his brain and rests in stillness (sound familiar?).
- All over the world, people have discovered their own paths to self-knowledge, self-mastery, balance, vitality, and contentment, whether they choose yoga, journaling, prayer, or simple breathing exercises to do so.

→ What could mindful, conscious self-discipline look like in *your* life?

TAKE ACTION:

Here's a practical plan for helping you bring more self-discipline into your life through meditation.

Step 1: Choose Your Meditation Technique

You need something to sharpen your focus. To begin training the mind, you need to give it deliberate structure and form. A mindfulness practice is something you diligently return to when you're distracted or tired—it's not the practice itself that holds value but your repeated efforts to focus on it.

- You can choose a daily mindfulness meditation focusing on the breath, or you can choose a more free-form Shikantaza approach.
- Use writing, reading, and contemplation, or build in some meditative elements in your prayer.
- You can build a mindfulness discipline into movement, such as with a daily walk, swimming, or yoga.
- Even dancing and singing or chanting can be meditative if you treat them as practices to which you continuously bring your focus.

Choose something that is appealing to your temperament but which will also challenge you. Mantras, affirmations, and guided meditations, for example, are great for stress reduction, but are they strengthening your self-discipline? Have the courage to assign yourself a task that will challenge you to grow.

Step 2: Schedule, Prioritize, and Commit

Once you've carefully discerned the form you'd like your meditative discipline to take, it's time to commit to it by agreeing with yourself that you will practice every day, no excuses.

Simply see meditation as a non-negotiable part of life. Even if you are sad, bored, confused, or angry, that's fine—bring that to your meditation practice, and that will be your work for the day.

➜ Internalize the fact that *there are no conditions whatsoever that should prevent you from your practice.*

➜ You may need to meditate for a shorter period or in unfamiliar locations, but once you commit, know that that's it—you're doing it.

The benefit of meditation comes from the serenity, balance, and self-knowledge it creates, but part of it is simply turning up to the practice every day, no matter what.

If you are feeling especially resistant one day, meditate and then check in to see how you feel afterward.

• What happens when you embrace resistance and "surf" it out, rather than allowing it to dictate your actions?

• Can you see how excuses, fears, and irritations are just as fleeting and temporary as the itch on your nose you sometimes get when you're doing Zazen?

If you find yourself saying things like, "I don't have the time," then realize that this is an excuse. It's also a golden opportunity to get real with yourself and remember what you're trying to achieve, and why. You don't have to meditate for hours and become enlightened by Thursday.

But *consistency is key.*

Small, repeated steps will get you there faster than wanting overnight success or instant transformation.

Step 3: Ramp It Up

- If this were a book on *self-care*, *anxiety management*, or *stress relief*, then there would be no need to keep increasing the amount of time spent meditating.
- But since this is a book on *self-discipline*, and since we know that willpower is a muscle that grows stronger the more we use it, **we must keep pushing ourselves.**

Caveat: We are still mindful that meditation is goalless, and that we are proceeding without judgment, shame, force, or expectations. What we are doing, though, is recognizing that development is a process, and that to build our self-discipline, *we need to adjust our challenge as we improve.*

- You don't have to go crazy.
- You don't have to be slack about it, either.
- ➜ Find that middle path.

If things don't go as you expected, be quick to let it go and move on. You are never competing with anyone or trying to prove yourself; it is more that you are like a child learning to ride a bike, and to help your budding ability, you are gradually removing the training wheels and going a little faster...

Let your higher, wiser self be in charge, rather than your fearful ego.

Notice when you are in a state of mind where you are:

- Complaining
- Doubting
- Arguing
- Criticizing
- Justifying instant gratification

Notice and just smile at it all—it's only your ego, and you don't have to go along with it.

Be patient.

Don't take yourself too seriously.

➜ **Remember: The obstacle isn't in the way of the path. It IS the path.**

Step 4: Stay Alive

What you want to avoid is automatic, mindless action that is done out of habit.

Having a meditation discipline can sometimes get us trapped in a rut where we are only going through the motions.

Your activity is to:

- Constantly encounter reality—*fresh and utterly new in each moment.*
- Be vibrant and spontaneous with your practice.

- Occasionally try to mix things up.
- Don't make assumptions. About anything.
- Importantly, don't be too quick to assume you've mastered everything and can sit back and relax!
- Try out different forms of meditation now and then.

There is no end point to meditation, so you are never "finished." When something difficult or awkward arises, instead of ignoring it or fleeing, turn and face it instead and become curious about what you don't yet know or understand, or what you don't feel in control of.

These small things are like doors you can open, expanding and deepening your practice. Don't merely sit on a cushion and act the part of someone meditating.

Instead, sit down, every moment, *as though you have never sat down before* and as though the moment you are discovering right now is bright, sparkly, and astonishingly new to you—because it is!

- Some days, the brave and challenging thing to do will be to push through resistance and strong negative emotion.
- Some days, the challenge will be to trust yourself enough to go silent and simply be, at rest in the moment.

Learning to discern between these things is what the adventure of meditation is all about. If you can keep up the challenge and stay on your toes, you will bring this alert frame of mind to everything you do in life, away from the meditation cushion.

You may start to look at obligations that would have made you procrastinate in the past as interesting new opportunities.

What to Do in the Face of Temptation, Distraction, or Strong Emotion

It's not *if* but *when*.

You **will** encounter something that wants to knock you off the path of conscious self-determination.

Guess what?

It's *now* that your real meditation practice kicks in.

Like a Shaolin monk who has been training kung Fu for decades and is finally facing a formidable enemy, you are tasked with taking the discipline you've cultivated and using it.

➡ **Be grateful for temptations and distractions! They are the iron against which you sharpen your self-discipline and free will.**

The enemy can take many forms:

- Lack of self-belief: "Oh, I just don't have any self-discipline!"
- Fear: "If I try, I'll only fail, anyway."
- Laziness: "If it ain't broke, don't fix it!"
- Lack of clarity: "Hm, I don't know... Maybe... What was the question?"
- Value incongruity: "I know I should do this, but I just don't *care*."
- Distractibility: "I will, but later. I'm busy now!"
- And on and on...

What meditation can teach you, however, is that ALL of your excuses, fears, resistances, hindrances, weaknesses, and so on are irrelevant.

If you have practiced standing apart from and outside of your sensations and perceptions, you realize you can also do this with *any* unhelpful core belief, *any* old narrative, *any* emotion, *any* self-sabotaging thought. You can see that these illusions your mind creates are just as flimsy and intransient as hearing a dog barking next door.

Self-discipline gives you options. Yes, you are tempted and distracted and emotional and irrational. But regardless, what do you want to do? What path do you want to be on, and why? Self-discipline is what allows you to get on and travel that path!

Scenario 1:

It's time to go to the gym, but you think, "Boo! I don't want to. I'm tired."

And once you settle down on the sofa and see that it's drizzling outside, you start to actually believe your own story that you are, in fact, too tired. You don't see your self-talk as excuses but observations.

- You don't see the fear, stubbornness, or passivity that is really behind your current state.
- You don't see the choice you've just made or the opportunity you've passed up on.
- You might even tell yourself and others a very convincing tale: "Oh, it's a rest day for me today! I'm doing self-care."

You stay at home, life goes on as it always has, and three years later, when you see someone in great shape, you feel a pang of jealousy—but in your lack of self-awareness and integrity, you cannot even recognize the reason for this jealousy.

"Oh, well, it's easy for him. He's young and has a fast metabolism. He should try looking like that with my genes!"

→ Lack of self-discipline and lack of self-awareness go hand in hand, creating a life that is never really all it could be.

Scenario 2:

It's time to go to the gym, but you think, "Boo! I don't want to. I'm tired."

Because you've been meditating daily and taking control of your own mental state, you see this bit of self-talk for exactly what it is: fear and laziness. Nothing more. Because you've had a lot of practice observing and noticing thoughts and feelings, you don't instantly engage with, believe, or follow every thought.

- Even though you feel resistance, you go to the gym, anyway.
- You calmly notice that the resistance evaporates.
- Around ten minutes into training, and when you leave, you're actually energized and confident.

Getting yourself to the gym is sometimes easy and sometimes not, but whatever knee-jerk thoughts your brain presents, it's your *reason and will* that make the final decision.

→ One day, a friend you haven't seen in three years is astonished to see how much progress you've made, and you feel proud in the knowledge that this is an outcome that you created for yourself.

In the classic kids' cartoons, there's always a little devil on one shoulder and a little angel on the other, and we see the protagonist struggling to decide who to listen to. But mindfulness is a way to calmly take a step away from this battle and refuse to keep pushing and pulling, guilting, and shaming.

Instead of being the tormented cartoon character, we put ourselves in the position of *viewer and director* of the cartoon, able to say to ourselves, **"I'm experiencing temptation right now, but I have a choice."**

Chapter Takeaways:

- Zen's non-intellectual and non-rational spiritual practice helps with self-discipline since the approach is about cultivating conscious awareness—the bedrock for any deliberate and self-directed action. Meditation builds discipline, but it also requires discipline. Focused mindful awareness is both the result of self-discipline and its cause.
- Zazen is goal-less sitting meditation, where we encounter reality without symbols, clinging, or resistance. Meditation helps discipline because in awareness, we can choose whether to engage in momentary distractions or not.
- Shikantaza is "just being," or meditation without an object. Nature contemplation can help foster shikantaza.
- For Shaolin monks, finding meaning and purpose in life is the only real goal, and finding the path in a world filled with illusion is the real challenge. There are five hindrances on the way: sensual desire, ill will (negative emotions), dullness (laziness), restlessness (distraction), and doubt. Recognize, accept, observe, and gain

distance from these impediments when you become aware of them.

- Meditation opens a brief window of awareness; in that window, we can remind ourselves to be better and to do better. Choose a technique, schedule it, and consistently challenge yourself to go further, never getting stuck in a rut. Be grateful for temptations and distractions! They are the iron against which you sharpen your self-discipline and free will.

Chapter 8: How Action Changes Your Mindset

Awareness matters, and so does action.

Nothing becomes real in our world until we take action and make it so.

In this chapter, we'll look at the attitudes that are necessary to consistently take positive action... as well as the trap we can fall into when we act unconsciously, or else keep making one false start after another.

What It Really Means to Have a "Can-Do" Attitude

"You have to have a positive attitude!"

People say this, and it's glib and cliché, but it also happens to be true.

➔ A major mistake that people make when trying to create the lives they want for themselves is thinking that state of mind is a result of external events.

➔ This is backward: Your state of mind is a cause of external events.

With a negative attitude, you are **passive**, and life is something out there that happens to you whether you like it or not.

With a positive attitude, you are **active** and make things happen because those things matter to you and because you trust in your power to make them real.

That a positive can-do attitude is associated with a self-disciplined life and more success is obvious. But to actually make the mindset shift is something that too few of us commit to. It's a practice and something we have to continuously choose to do—nobody can force us to use our own agency!

Growth Mindset Versus Fixed Mindset

Consider the example of Muhammed Ali, who is today known as one of the world's greatest boxers. In her 2006 book *Mindset*, author Carol Dweck says of Ali:

> "[He] was not a natural. He had great speed, but he didn't have the physique of a great fighter, he didn't have the strength, and he didn't have the classical moves. In fact, he boxed all wrong. He didn't block punches with his arms and elbows. He punched in rallies like an amateur. He kept his jaw exposed. He pulled back his torso to evade the impact of oncoming punches, which Jose Torres [former colleague of Ali] said was 'like someone in the middle of a train track trying to avoid being hit by an oncoming train, not by moving to one or the other side of the track, but by running backwards.'"

Yet despite all this, he consistently beat opponents who did things right, had the right stats, and were theoretically bigger, better, and stronger.

The reason? His mindset.

You only need to look at a photo of Ali or watch footage of him in a match to see something striking: Despite his fairly average measurements and modest physique, he won 56 of 61 fights in his career, some against boxers far more skilled than he was.

According to Dweck, Ali had what she calls a **growth mindset**.

A **growth mindset** is the belief that who we are now isn't all we'll ever be, and that growth and development are possible.

- Because we believe that skills can be acquired, we trust that we can always improve.
- That implies that failure and challenge are to be embraced because they help us become better.
- We acknowledge that effort is essential to building mastery, and so embrace it, welcoming feedback without letting our egos get in the way, and facing setbacks with resilience and curiosity.
- The growth mindset is, in other words, the proverbial *can-do* attitude.

The **fixed mindset** is the opposite. It sees human characteristics as fixed and unchangeable (something you're born with—or cursed with!).

- Because of that belief, challenges are best avoided and feedback ignored to protect the ego.
- Effort is not seen as essential, and so none is made.
- Instead, the person may resort to blame, defensiveness, and giving up.

The aptitude you are actually born with? It's not all that important—it's what you *do* with it that counts.

Your success, then, is about:

- How you respond to setbacks.
- How you frame your own learning.
- The way you think about effort.

In sum, it comes down to attitude.

Can't-do: "I'm not good right now, so I'll never be."

Can-do: "I can learn. I can find a way."

Can't-do: "Failure is painful, and I hate it. I'll do anything to avoid it."

Can-do: "I can handle failure. It has something to teach me, and I want to learn."

Can't-do: "I'm not good enough."

Can-do: "How can I be good enough? What can I do right now?"

Again, it all comes down to conscious *action*—and that requires our self-discipline.

BE AWARE: Do you tell yourself, "That's just the way I am," or assume that you can never achieve certain goals because you just don't have what it takes?

Be really clear about these self-imposed limits and try a little trick: Add "right now" or "yet" onto the end of these statements. "I'm not good at math... yet." Or "I'm struggling... right now."

Congruence Versus Incongruence

A big part of the can-do attitude is integrity.

- **Being congruent** = all parts of yourself are in agreement and alignment. Your thoughts, your feelings, and your actions are all part of the same whole.

- **Being incongruent** = some part of you is not quite on board with the other parts.

For example, you meditate daily and have become more aware of your thought patterns, and you have allowed your rational conscious mind to make healthy decisions for you.

Both your thoughts and actions are both pulling in a positive direction—and yet things don't improve for you. Why? Because your *emotions* have been left behind. You might rationally understand something to be the case and behave as you think you should, but in truth, your heart is just not in it.

There is a lack of congruence.

Or perhaps your thoughts and emotions are both positive and aligned well, but you fail to achieve the success you want because your *actions* haven't caught up and reflect the changes you think and feel.

Famed author Brene Brown explains in her 2015 book *Rising Strong* how alignment between thoughts, feelings, and actions is like having a stool with all three legs strong and stable—without one of the three legs, the stool is wobbly or entirely useless.

How do we make sure that we think positive, feel positive, and act positive?

TAKE ACTION:

- **When you learn something new, find a way to apply it**. Take action according to your new understanding. This takes it outside of the realm of purely intellectual and makes it real in your world.
- **When you act, take time to process the results on an emotional and cognitive level**. How do you feel? Are there any updates to your self-concept that you need to make?
- **When you are aware of an emotion, be curious about how it interacts with your thoughts and behaviors**. Without shame or judgment, investigate the thoughts and actions that came before and after the feeling. By embedding your feelings in the bigger picture, you get a more three-dimensional view on your current situation.

Example: During a meditation session, you notice how you keep fidgeting with your hands and feet (a behavior). Instead of just thinking, "I should stop fidgeting," and forcing yourself to stop, you investigate the feelings and thoughts behind this action. You see that you're feeling nervous and on edge, and the thought patterns behind that go along the lines of, "You're getting this wrong. You're a loser, and you need to fix it fast."

In your meditation session and beyond, you *work on all three*—thoughts, feelings, and behaviors.

In time, you:

- Change the underlying thought pattern (thoughts).
- You feel more relaxed (feelings).
- You stop fidgeting quite so much (behaviors).

The "problem" was solved not because you had enough self-discipline to force a change, but rather because that change was a *holistic* one.

- Thoughts, feelings, and actions all influence one another.
- That means that a change in one necessitates a change in another.

If you are not aligned and whole in this way, you keep on telling yourself, "Stop fidgeting, dammit!" but the thoughts and feelings involved are never addressed, and so you just keep on fidgeting. So though we talk about a "mindset" and attitude, the changes need to happen on more than just a cognitive level—they need to be complete.

Saboteur Versus Sage

In 2012, Psychologist Shirzad Chamine put forward a theory of human development called "positive intelligence." He claimed that our success in life comes down to our degree of **positive intelligence**.

Positive intelligence = the ratio of how much time we spend listening to our inner Saboteur versus our inner Sage.

- The inner **Saboteur**:
  - This is the voice of self-criticism, doubt, fear, and judgement.
  - Ultimately, this voice is trying to keep us safe, but it does so by undermining us and twisting our perception.
  - This voice is based in the past and future and is negative, fearful, and judgmental.

- The inner **Sage:**
  - This voice is the calmer, kinder voice of reason.
  - This voice speaks from a place of empowerment, curiosity, creativity, and contentment.
  - This voice is based squarely in the present and is optimistic, rational, and open.

Every moment of the day, you're talking to yourself. Is this the voice of the Sage or the Saboteur?

The Saboteur says, "You're stupid," but the Sage says, "Hey, everyone makes mistakes. You're learning."

Your positive intelligence, according to Chamine, is determined by which of these voices you follow and the extent to which you allow them to shape your world.

Good Versus Perfect

A can-do attitude isn't about waiting around for the ideal circumstances before you give yourself permission to act.

Some facts:

- There is no perfect time (or rather, the perfect time is always the same: *now*).
- We will never be 100% ready, and there will never be a chance to act that contains a 100% chance of success with 0% risk.
- The right attitude therefore is one that doesn't "let the perfect be the enemy of the good."

A particularly sneaky form of resistance is when we tell ourselves we will act—but only later. We'll do it someday, when we've done more research and we're better prepared so we can do it *right*.

But this is just passivity wearing the disguise of proactivity. As we saw in an earlier section, you learn by doing. Just start and work it out as you go along.

Let go of the pressure to "do your best" and focus on being all you can be.

All you have to do is:

- Turn up and take action.
- Assess your results.
- Adjust.
- Act again.

The outcome will take care of itself if you just focus on conscious action right now. *The perfect is made up of many tiny moments of imperfection!*

A can-do attitude, therefore, is one that is based on growth, that is congruent in all parts of the self, that is guided by the voice of the Sage rather than the Saboteur, and which is focused on action, even if that action isn't always perfect.

Whatever comes your way, you **can do** it.

Success =

- 10% the circumstances you're dealt.
- 90% what you choose to *do* with that.

TAKE ACTION: Right now, how are you doing emotionally?

Are you more in a fixed mindset or a growth mindset?

Is the Sage running the show or the Saboteur?

Identify one thing you're feeling like you can't do at the moment and challenge yourself to look at it from the opposite frame of mind.

<u>The Mindset of a Winner</u>

One of the most fascinating mental frames to study is that of a winner.

You might ask yourself:

- What energizes some people to pursue their goals?
- What allows some of us to walk paths others couldn't dream of and travel further along those paths than we even thought possible?
- Why do some people keep going and going long after everyone else has given up?

You've probably guessed that the answer is—**winners have a unique mindset**.

In this chapter, we'll explore what this mindset is. But first of all, let's clarify what a "winner" is. We're not just talking about people who fit the narrow conventional standards for success like extreme wealth or celebrity status.

Rather, a winner is someone who, *in their own unique way*,

- Applies their will.
- Achieves their intentions.
- Executes their plans with a high degree of excellence.

No matter their age, their station in life, their background, their limitations, or the sphere of life they focus their energy on, these are the people who make things happen.

And keeping in mind what we learned about growth and fixed mindsets, remember that **winners are not born, but made**.

Being a winner is not something you are gifted with, but something you choose and cultivate every day, every moment. This is great news because it means you never have to resign yourself to the life you have and assume that others have something you don't. Every day, the winner's mindset can be yours... if you're willing to cultivate it.

Here's how:

Know With Crystal Clarity What You Want to Achieve

You need clarity of vision and you need a goal, but that goal needs to be congruent and speak to your values. If you know what you want, you'll know it when you find it, and you'll know more quickly when you're wasting time on things that don't get you there. You'll create a plan that focuses you and identifies your priorities— and with the right plan, you don't need luck!

Take Responsibility for Achieving It

Here's a challenge: Honestly ask yourself right now who you are currently blaming for something.

- Maybe you're blaming your parents for your lousy money habits.
- Maybe you're blaming your bosses for your low salary.
- Maybe you're blaming the weather for the fact that you haven't gone for a walk today.

Take a close look at this blame and see if you cannot reclaim some of your responsibility:

- Even if your parents didn't teach you about budgeting, does that mean you can't learn now?
- Even if you have no control over what your bosses pay you, don't you have control to negotiate a pay raise or look for another job?
- And if you're not going for your walk, isn't it at least partly because *you've* decided you don't want to?

When you take responsibility, you open your eyes to the action you *can* take. And when you take action, you gain the control necessary to change your situation.

Sign up for an adult financial literacy class.

Start looking for another job.

Invest in a raincoat so that you can do your daily walk even if it's raining!

Sometimes when you say:

> *"I can't change anything. It's not up to me. It's not my fault. It's out of my hands."*

What you're really saying is:

> *"I've given up my own power to change this situation."*

That doesn't mean that you are "to blame," either—remove blame and shame and judgment from the picture entirely.

You made a mistake? That's fine. Own it and move on.

What can you do better next time? Shame is not useful, especially when it distracts you from taking positive action.

Forget About Other People's Goals

A big part of being congruent and living to your own values is realizing a key principle:

→ **You are running your own race and don't need to compete against others.**

How other people are dealing with their challenges, what they have decided to value, and how far along they are on the path is entirely irrelevant to you.

Winners "stay in their lane."

- They don't get distracted by other people in their lanes.
- They don't interfere with others or judge them.
- At the same time, they don't let the interference or judgment of others keep them from *their* path.

Their motivation is not the approval of others or compliance with convention. They set their own standards and then focus on that.

Now, that doesn't mean they don't learn from others or get inspired by them. But this is never an attitude of comparison, but rather, "Wow, you're striving for your goals, and so am I—what can we teach one another?"

Ironically, the people who most strongly identify with terms like "winner" and its inverse, "loser," may be the least able to hold a winner's mindset since they believe that there is only one way to win first place.

Assume Effort is Non-Negotiable and Constant

Another irony is that even though winners *do* achieve, they spend most of their time not enjoying the reward of their hard work but... working hard.

Think about it: The person who crosses the finish line gets a glorious moment of achievement and pride at the end. But before those few seconds, they were working diligently and consistently day after day.

For hours, days, weeks.

Maybe years.

We only see the impressive end result. We *don't* see:

- The daily grind.
- The endless patience.
- The boring days of training.
- The consistent effort done no matter what, without praise or recognition.

Winners don't argue with the fact that hard work is required. It's non-negotiable. They do it because they're in for the long haul, and that's that. Instead of imagining the dreamy finish line and getting discouraged about how far they still have to go, they put their head down and make it happen.

Don't Settle

Average is fine. It's okay. There's nothing wrong with being like everyone else.

But when it comes to something that *really* matters to a winner, average is simply not enough. Winners don't settle for good enough—if they can do more, they do more.

→ If you are honest with yourself, how many times have you settled in with a mediocre result just because it was easy to do so and because nobody challenged you to go further?

When you have a winner's mindset, you sometimes find yourself wanting to keep going long after other people are satisfied, and they cannot understand your vision or why you'd want to put in the effort.

For winners, following their own heart is always more satisfying than following the crowd. They hold their own standards and don't let themselves off the hook even if it's convenient.

Don't settle, and be honest with yourself if you're taking the easy route.

Take risks.

After all, at the end of your life, *you* are the only one who has to be content with the decisions you've made or haven't made.

Stay Open

A winner possesses a certain kind of creativity—a feeling of the world being filled with limitless possibilities. When you believe in your own self-efficacy and you're willing to work, suddenly everywhere you look you see opportunity.

When something doesn't pan out, you simply get curious about what *does*. It's like you are wearing rose-tinted glasses, but in this case, the glasses only allow you to see the new, the possible, the hopeful, the exciting. This kind of flexibility means you are open to adapting the plan for how you achieve your goals. You don't give up; you just adjust.

Let's boil it all down.

Being a winner is not about luck or being given opportunities by others. It's about two things:

1)   The way you see the world
2)   The action you take as a result of that mindset

And what's more encouraging than knowing that both of these things are available to anyone right now?

BE AWARE: Forget about everyone else for a second and get real with your own conscience. Look at what you could be doing better at in life and rise to the challenge of meeting better goals—not for anyone else, but for you.

Even if you're not quite sure what to do next, as a first step, at least acknowledge to yourself that there is some potential you may be leaving unfulfilled.

Back at Square One? Navigating the "Yo-Yo Effect"

You can probably already guess what phenomenon the term "yo-yo effect" refers to, and chances are, you've experienced it yourself.

Duke University psychologist Kelly D. Brownell defines it as cyclic weight loss and weigh gain due to dieting or calorie restriction. Dr. Brownell suggests that people usually tend not to sustain a diet and more often than not revert to old eating patterns.

You know the story:

1. You make a change to your diet, and you lose weight.
2. You think, "Phew! Job's done," and revert to your old eating habits.
3. You gain weight.
4. You go around the loop again.

Or it may go another way:

1. You make a change to your diet but don't lose weight.
2. You think, "Oh no!" and get depressed and discouraged, and so revert to your old eating habits.
3. You gain weight.
4. You go around the loop again.

As you can see, whichever way it plays out, you are on a rollercoaster of extreme emotions and unsustainable lifestyle changes. You can make changes, but you can't get them to *stick*.

→ It's almost as though what you are training yourself to do is start... but not finish.

Consider that at a certain high weight, you require X number of calories. When you restrict calories, you lose weight, and along with that weight loss comes a reduced caloric need. In other words, it takes fewer calories to maintain a smaller body than it does a bigger one. No, your metabolism hasn't slowed down and you haven't entered "starvation mode"—your body has just changed.

But if your new, smaller body requires fewer calories, and you suddenly eat X number of calories again, well, you will return to your starting weight. You made a *temporary* change to your behavior, and so your success was also temporary.

The underlying problem causing yo-yo dieting is not broken metabolisms, but mindsets, i.e., thinking that a diet is a temporary solution that, once you reach a degree of success, can be abandoned so you can go back to your old ways.

If you think of your behavior changes as only temporary tricks and hacks to get the result you want, you're dooming yourself to relapse.

- "Diets" don't work because they are by their nature *temporary*.
- *Permanent* lifestyle change is what helps people lose weight and keep it off.

To be on a diet is a mental state that is actually counterproductive.

You imagine that you are demonstrating some supernatural self-control for a definite purpose. You see what you're doing as somehow outside of normal life and different from your "normal" way of doing things.

But to make real changes, you need to revamp your entire idea of normal and change the way you think about self-control—*it is not something you do so that you earn the right to not have to do it later.*

When you are on a diet, you think:

- This is going to be tough, so I'll have my fun this weekend and start on Monday.
- I've been on this diet for three whole weeks now, so I've earned the right to some junk food now!

Can you see the problem?

You have a mindset that says that bad behavior is the normal state of affairs and a "treat," whereas healthy, disciplined behavior is something unpleasant to get over and done with as soon as possible.

This is the reason so many nutritionists and health experts say that "95% of diets fail." That's what they're designed to do! Until you can say...

- I consciously choose to live a happy and healthy life, and
- The better I do, the more encouraged I am to keep going and doing more

... then you are going to be stuck on the merry-go-round, the rollercoaster, or the yo-yo.

Naturally, the yo-yo effect is not just about dieting and weight loss, but about any attempt to genuinely alter behavior for good.

- You don't train for weeks and complete several marathons and then quit and become sedentary, hoping to keep your toned figure.

- You don't turn up to a new job, work hard for a month, and then slack forever more and expect to earn your salary all the same.
- You don't quit smoking for a month and then reward yourself by taking up the habit again, confident that your lung cancer risk is now permanently reduced.

Instead, at your new level of success, you need to adjust your expectations and maintain the new, adjusted level of effort.

Example: If you weigh 600 pounds, you can lose vast amounts of weight on a daily diet of 4000 calories. But as you get closer to a healthier body weight, you will reach a point where you have to eat far less than 4000 calories—which is, after all, an amount that others would gain on. The fact that after one year of dieting you are eating a tiny fraction of what you used to eat is not because you have harmed your body's metabolism; it's because you've had to adjust and eat like a person with a smaller body does.

This trajectory is the same for any endeavor in life.

If you are expecting to keep on making the same level of effort, or even to drop back down to a previous level of low effort, then you cannot be surprised when your rewards reflect that and diminish as well.

- → When you achieve or make any small advance, you place yourself at a new level.
- → To stay at this level, you need to *continue* to behave like someone at this level.
- → When you behave like someone at a lower level, that is where you will end up.

The mistake is always to revert to old habits.

Changing Your Life One Action at a Time, One Belief at a Time

Let's dig a little deeper into the *process* of change. **When we develop, improve, and grow, it is seldom a simple linear process.** When we lose weight, for example, it is not just the number on the scale that changes.

- The way we behave changes.
- The way we think changes.
- Our entire identity changes.

You may occasionally see someone who has lost immense amounts of weight, who nevertheless still dresses in too-big clothes or turns side-on when walking through doorways. Their physical body has changed, but their identity has not yet caught up.

As we saw in the previous section, we can often fail to make changes or to *maintain* those changes because we engage only in temporary solutions while keeping our attitudes, lifestyle, and habits exactly the same.

Your beliefs drive your behavior.

If you only change the behavior and not the underlying beliefs, that behavior change will always be temporary.

There are three layers of behavior change:

1. A change in your *outcomes*.
2. A change in your *beliefs*.
3. A change in your *identity*.

BE AWARE: Right now, think about a long-term goal that you have, and write it down. Then look carefully at the way you have phrased it and ask what level of change it addresses.

You might think, "I want to lose ten pounds," or, "I want to learn to speak French."

These are great goals, but they are superficial—they concern the outward final outcome only (number 1). They say nothing about the underlying beliefs (number 2) or identity (number 3) that would have to accompany such a change.

So:

→ **Your behavior is driven by beliefs.**
→ **Your beliefs are influenced by your identity.**
→ **But to complete the loop, your identity is also influenced by your behavior.**

The habitual behaviors that you engage in are a reflection of what you believe, and these come down to who you think you are.

Example: If you eat healthy and wholesome foods every day, it's because you believe in the value of doing so, and these beliefs stem from the identity of, "I'm a healthy person." Your identity, beliefs, and behaviors all work to reinforce one another. Every day that you eat healthy, you confirm to yourself your identity and cement your beliefs.

But, you may instead only make superficial behavioral changes—for example, forcing yourself to have a fruit smoothie every morning for breakfast. If this behavior is accompanied by a belief that healthy eating is a boring chore and the identity that "I'll always be an unhealthy person," then nothing will change in the long term.

In fact, one way or another, your *real* identity and core beliefs will eventually assert themselves, and your behavior will reflect that.

➜ **If we want to make lasting changes, we need to make changes on all three levels.**

One of the problems with making change stick is that it takes time for people to update their new identities to match their new behaviors.

Example:

- You've been eating poorly your whole life. In other words, you have lots of evidence for your *identity* as an unhealthy eater, and your old *behaviors* and *beliefs* followed along with that.
- But then you decide you want to change and eat better. You start making some behavioral changes. These changes are good and are having a positive impact. You are on your way to having a new identity as a healthy eater—but you're not there yet!
- One day, you're faced with the choice of eating in an unhealthy way again.

At this point, where are you?

➜ You have lots of evidence to suggest that you're an unhealthy eater, but relatively little evidence to suggest that you're a healthy eater. Likewise, you may still hold all the beliefs you had that matched your "unhealthy eater" self-concept and haven't quite internalized the new and improved beliefs that come with a healthy lifestyle.

So what happens now?

- Momentum and habit win out, and you behave in accordance with your beliefs and identity—and make the unhealthy choice.
- You may even feel better after such a choice—after all, everything is now in alignment and back to being familiar again, right?

Change is possible, but it takes time.

Every experience you have changes who you are, and every action you take is one more step toward creating the person you are. But this doesn't happen all at once.

Example: You may go to a French language class, and that's a great thing, and go again the next week, and the week after that. But it may take *months or years* of classes for you to start feeling and acting like a French speaker.

That doesn't mean that the single class is worthless, though. With **repeated actions** in a new direction, the changes do gradually take root and become more and more real for you.

- Every choice reinforces a new set of beliefs and a new identity.
- No single act or choice will change you from A to B.
- However, many single acts done on a consistent basis *will* change you.

Progress will be slow, but it is sure.

This is why self-discipline is so important—it helps us keep taking action in that period where we are no longer our old selves but we are not quite our new selves yet, either.

→ **Discipline helps you make "microevolutions"** with every choice you make.

We change who we are by changing what we do, but our ability to change what we do also depends on our ability to start thinking of who we are in a different way. A good trick is to remind yourself of the value of small, consistent actions done regularly.

- Every time you make a healthy choice, pause and tell yourself, "I am a heathy eater. I love veggies. I always choose wisely and prefer wholesome food."
- Every time you go to the gym, pause and say, "I'm a gym goer. I'm one of those people who exercises daily."
- Every time you pick up your paintbrush, tell yourself, "I'm an artist. I'm a creative person."

And yes, say these things even if it's the first time you're doing the actions! Because you are not just changing your behavior. You're changing:

- Your beliefs
- Your attitudes
- Your feelings
- The entire way you think about yourself

You don't just want to act like a new person. You want to genuinely **be** that new person.

Nobody's perfect, and we all mess up. So, when your behavior is a step backward and you choose the old habit, do the inverse and say, "This is *not* the person I am. This is *not* the kind of thing I do." Consciously tell yourself that this behavior is not evidence for your old identity, but a temporary diversion that can be ignored.

Imagine that someone offers two people a cigarette.

- The first person says, "No thanks, I'm trying to quit."
- The second person says, "No thanks, I don't smoke."

The first person has made a behavioral change but not an identity change. The second person has made both kinds of changes. The first is essentially saying, "I'm a smoker who is temporarily behaving like a non-smoker."

The first person is changing their behavior and hoping that this in time will change how they think and feel, and ultimately, one day in the distant future, they'll be someone different, i.e., a non-smoker.

The second person is making changes in a completely different direction. They *start* with a change in identity, then hope that this change will ripple out through their thoughts and feelings and finally in their outward behavior.

TAKE ACTION:

Try this simple two-step process to make the sometimes-awkward change from A to B:

1. Decide on the person you want to be.
2. PROVE it to yourself in small ways.

For example, decide that you want to be a painter and then prove that you *are* a painter by making one small choice, right now, today, that is the kind of thing a painter would do.

Think about the person you want to be and then ask, "What would they choose right now?"

New identities require new evidence—so find that evidence. Before you decide what to do or how to do it, decide the **who**—what kind of a person do you want to be? Think of the life you want to lead and ask, "What kind of a person must I be to live that life?"

Identities take time to change, but they are not permanent. With conscious and self-disciplined choice, they can take a different shape. In time, your identity will catch up and you will think of yourself in a completely new way. When this happens, congratulations—you have made a breakthrough and accessed the kind of life change that will *last*.

<u>"Pavloving" Yourself</u>

In the 1890s, physiologist Ivan Pavlov discovered in his experiments that dogs would salivate in anticipation of receiving their food. He found that if he paired their mealtimes with the ringing of a bell, he could get the dogs to salivate simply by ringing the bell alone, even in the absence of food.

He thus paired the two stimuli together and conditioned the dogs' behavioral response.

Ever since, psychologists have wondered if it's possible to "Pavlov yourself" and essentially condition your own responses. Because the brain is plastic (it has neuroplasticity) and able to adapt, the answer is *yes*.

➔ **Classical conditioning is a way of learning that happens automatically and unconsciously.**

It happens because of the *associations* we form (in the Pavlov experiment, the dogs associated the sound of the bell with food). Classical conditioning is always happening in our everyday lives, but that doesn't mean we can't have a degree of control over it for our own benefit.

Example: Let's say you're a smoker who always has a smoke break in the outside patio at your workplace. One day, you walk through this area to collect a delivery and suddenly feel the urge for a cigarette.

This is because your brain has *associated* this particular patio with having a cigarette. Now, you may have no conscious control over this process, but you *can* manipulate it: If you decided you wanted to stop smoking, you could deliberately avoid going near that area to try to break the association and reduce temptation for yourself.

By the same token, therapists use a form of classical conditioning to help people overcome phobias or PTSD responses (by pairing a fear-inducing stimulus with positive feelings, for example).

Classical conditioning can be used to break bad habits so that we can form new and better ones.

We can *consciously* decide to manage our environment so that our *unconscious* reactions and responses are optimized. Here's how.

TAKE ACTION:

Step 1: Identify the bad habit that you want to "decondition".

For example, it may be that you have a bad habit of rummaging through the cupboards after dinner each night to snack on cookies and candy.

Step 2: Notice when this behavior occurs, and what precedes and co-occurs with it.

You take a close look at this behavior.

What triggers it for you?

Is the end of dinner the cue to start snacking?

No, because you notice that you snack, anyway, whether you've had dinner or not. You realize that the thought, "Hm, I wonder if there's something nice to snack on in the kitchen," comes reliably at around 8 p.m. every evening no matter what you're doing.

Step 3: Remove or alter those triggers and associations.

We cannot remove the trigger of it being 8 p.m., but we can modify it. In this case, maybe you decide that you'll take a walk after dinner every evening so that you are out of the house at that time every day.

Step 4: Make new associations

In time, your subconscious will start to associate 8 p.m. with being out of the house on a walk. If you wanted to, you could also re-condition any temptation to snack as a new stimulus, i.e., "Oh, I'm feeling like a snack—it must be getting close to my walk time!"

Another example: You identify a bad "habit," which is really a mild phobia in disguise—you avoid driving since having a near-fatal accident some years back. You have conditioned yourself so that every time you get into a car, you immediately start to panic.

In this case, the conditioned response is not a behavior like snacking or salivating, but rather an emotional reaction.

You decide to use classical conditioning to break this association. Just like in the previous section where we learned to slowly create evidence for a new identity, you break this association by slowly creating moments where being in a car *doesn't* fill you with anxiety.

The technique of "exposure therapy" is based on classical conditioning.

➜ The idea is simple: You expose yourself to a stimulus that ordinarily provokes fear, but pair it with relaxation instead.

Gradually, you break the association that *car = panic.*

How?

- First, you stand near to a car for a few minutes.
- The moment you feel yourself panicking, you stop and do a relaxation exercise, perhaps with breathing or visualization to calm you down again.
- You do this a few times until being near a car doesn't provoke any reaction.
- Then, you take another step. You get into the car, and when the panic sets in, you do your relaxation exercise again. You teach your brain that *car = relaxation.* You are giving yourself

evidence that your old associations are unfounded.

- Once you are comfortable with this, you sit in the car with the ignition turned on and do the same thing.
- Then you take a short one-minute drive.
- Then you increase that to a five-minute drive, and so on.
- In time, being in a car no longer causes you anxiety.

The great thing about including a classical conditioning element into your personal development efforts is that once the new associations are made, you don't *need* self-discipline anymore. You are simply doing the right thing on autopilot instead of the wrong thing!

➜ But you do need a little self-discipline to initially become aware of your conditioned responses and to consciously set up new patterns and associations for yourself.

Even if you don't have an obvious phobia to tackle or a serious snacking habit that needs attention, you can use the power of association to support good habits and make it harder to engage in bad ones:

- Have a work ritual to associate a certain action, location, or sensation with "time to work."
- Example: Sitting down with your morning coffee and turning on the monitor is always a sign that your workday has begun.
- Have a bedtime ritual that signals to your brain that it's time to relax and sleep.
- Example: Lighting a candle, reading something soothing, or meditating.

- Have set eating routines. If binge eating is a problem, you might have certain rituals that keep you on track.
  o Example: A single square of dark chocolate at the end of the day is the last thing you eat and a sign that you're done eating for the day.

Chapter Takeaways:

- Your state of mind is not a result of external events but a *cause* of external events. Being positive means being proactive, not passive.
- Having a "can-do" attitude is about having a growth rather than a fixed mindset ("I can learn; I can improve"); about congruence between thoughts, feelings, and actions (i.e., holistic integrity); about listening to the inner Sage rather than the inner Saboteur (developing "positive intelligence"); and about not letting the perfect be the enemy of the good.
- Study the winner's mindset: They come in all shapes and sizes, but winners make things happen, and they are made, not born. Cultivate a winner's mindset by clarifying your goals, taking responsibility to achieve them (i.e., not being a victim or blaming others), refraining from comparison or competition, working hard and consistently, having the courage to not settle for average, and staying open to possibilities and opportunities.
- Watch out for the yo-yo effect. If you think of your behavior changes as only temporary tricks and hacks to get the result you want, you're dooming

yourself to relapse. You cannot revert to old habits and expect to maintain any gains.

- "Pavlov" yourself to break bad habits so you can build better ones. Classical conditioning is a way of learning that happens automatically and unconsciously. Identify a bad habit and its triggers, remove those triggers, and deliberately re-condition new ones.

Chapter 9: Make Your Emotions Work for You

The person with self-discipline knows a secret:

➔ **You can choose how you want to feel.**

Feelings are a part of life.

They are powerful and can influence what we think, how we behave, what we want, and what we believe about ourselves.

While this is all true, emotions are not our *masters*. We can learn to honor and understand our emotions without letting them derail us, overwhelm us, or confuse us.

How to Develop Emotional Discipline

Being self-disciplined is not about having no emotions or dominating the emotions you have.

Rather, it's about realizing that your conscious will and rational intention are ultimately what win out.

Feeling our emotions, having self-awareness, and respecting our lived experience is all a part of learning how to channel our emotions and direct them in the ways *we* choose.

After all, emotions are a powerful source of motivation, meaning, and purpose—we *want* to have emotions. However, we need to have emotional discipline if we hope to use our emotions wisely.

Mastering Emotions

Step 1: Be aware

The next time you feel a strong emotion, try this:

- Pause and become aware.
- Try to see if you can identify the cause that triggered that emotion.
  - A trigger can be an external event or situation, or an internal event such as a thought, feeling, or memory.
- Next, try to find where this emotion is located in your body.
  - What do you feel and where do you feel it?
- Finally, take a look at the thoughts that come along with these sensations.
  - Perhaps a feeling of nervousness and panic is accompanied with the thought, "You had better do this perfectly, or else!"

You might need to examine the self-talk you're engaged in or the core beliefs that are activated.

Step 2: Reframe

Remember that you can choose how you feel. Some emotions will pop up spontaneously, but with awareness, you can choose whether or not to feed them. Once you are aware of an emotional reaction as a reaction, you can ask if you'd like to change it and see things differently.

➜ "Mental re-framing" = changing your perspective and challenging yourself to have a different view.

Emotions are not reality.

We can feel one way today and another way tomorrow.

Therefore, **while we have to be aware of and honor our emotions, we mustn't confuse them with an objective appraisal of reality.**

Emotions are more like colored filters placed over reality. Mental reframing is simply a matter of *asking if you want to look at reality through a different filter.*

Mastering your own emotions is always the same two-step process:

1. Become aware.
2. Then reframe.

But there are two related misconceptions that get in the way of doing this:

Misconception 1: Feeling an emotion means you must express it

Sometimes, strong and intense feelings seem to command our action and full participation. It's as though we say, "With a feeling this strong, I *have to* express it."

But that's not really true.

An emotion's intensity is *not* proof of its accuracy or its usefulness.

In recent years, there has been a big push for people to develop emotional intelligence and awareness of how they feel—but it is a mistake to assume that once we know how we feel, we are automatically obliged to act on it or allow that feeling to guide our decision-making.

Important: We never want to deny or avoid our emotions or feel ashamed for having them. But what we can do is:

o   Put emotions into context
o   Recognize their effects
o   Consciously choose how to respond to them after the fact

If you've just received critical feedback, you may be feeling intensely embarrassed and defensive. This is a valid emotion. But it's also not one that you should allow to run wild.

Without self-awareness and self-discipline, you could let this emotion push you to respond angrily and say something you regret. The other alternative? Thank the person for their feedback and take some time to process things. Then, you decide what to do with the information given to you, and gradually, that pang of embarrassment fades.

Misconception 2: Controlling your emotions means you're being "fake" or emotionally unhealthy

It is indeed a shame to suppress your real experience and live with inauthenticity. But mature self-regulation, emotional control, and self-mastery are about *balance*—it's about making sure that your emotions are in their proper place.

Think of emotions like you do hunger or thirst. These impulses are there for a reason and serve you well. But there is a time and a place to indulge them, and your appetites don't always lead you to the best possible choices.

Self-discipline is merely making a space for your rational, conscious mind to step in and have its say, too. Just as you do in meditation, watch emotions come and go. Then, make decisions and choose your actions according to your values and what you are trying to rationally achieve.

- Sometimes your emotions play an important role in pointing you in the right direction.
- Sometimes they threaten to derail and sabotage you.
- Sometimes they mean nothing at all.

With mindful awareness and *conscious control*, you can discern which is which.

Take fear as an example. Is fear "good" or "bad"? Well, it's neither. It just is what it is.

- **Situation 1:** You are attempting to do electrical DIY work on your house despite not knowing anything about it. You feel fear and think, "I don't know what I'm doing."
- **Situation 2:** At work, you're asked to give a presentation in front of a big crowd about your area of expertise. You feel fear and think, "I don't know what I'm doing."

In *both* situations, fear is a valid response. But whether this fear *helps* or *hinders* largely depends on your degree of emotional discipline and self-mastery.

If you are able to be aware of your emotional responses, you can ask what purpose they're currently serving, and reframe as necessary.

- So, when you look closely at your fear in situation 1, you realize that it's telling you something important: There's risk and danger ahead.
- In the same way, it's self-discipline that allows you to look at situation 2 and tell yourself, "This fear is not accurate or helpful. There's no threat. I'm not going to allow this fear to stop me from seizing good opportunities at work."

Emotional Kung Fu: The Art of Turning Negative Emotions to Your Advantage

In the self-defense art of kung fu, the aim is not to *fight* an attacker but to *redirect* their attack. In the same way, emotional kung fu is not about vanquishing our emotions but learning to *channel* them to our own advantage.

In our culture of "toxic positivity," we can begin to believe that any negativity or discomfort is a problem that requires an immediate solution, and that "bad feelings" are more or less like unwanted waste that serves no purpose.

→ **But not only are negative emotions inevitable, they can be useful and can be put to the service of your goals.**

A fascinating 2012 study at Olin University found that people who were comfortable experiencing a range of different emotions tended to demonstrate better well-being, while those who ignored, judged, or evaded negative feelings showed lower levels of well-being.

Jonathan Adler, the professor who led the study, claimed that,

> "Those participants who were making meaning out of their experiences with a mixture of happiness and sadness actually showed increases in their psychological well-being, compared to people who were just reporting sadness, just reporting happiness, or some other mixture of emotions. It seems that there is something to be gained for your mental health in taking both the good and the bad together."

When you ignore or run away from negative emotions, you could be missing out on a great source of potential benefits. After all, how many people look back in life and say that the greatest lessons, insights, and achievements came with challenging times and negative emotions?

We don't need to get rid of negative emotions—we can *transform* them.

What's more, overcoming adversity and moving from negative to positive may in fact result in more satisfaction and feelings of meaning than never experiencing the bad emotions in the first place.

Author of the 2014 book *The Myths of Creativity*, David Burkus advises us to,

> "Think of the negative emotion as fuel that you can burn on the path to creation. The negative

emotions might just help you dig deeper into the problem and find a solution your happier self would never have uncovered."

Adversity, if worked on by the conscious will, can be re-christened as a growth opportunity and point of transformation. It's the old "blessing in disguise" idea!

The paradox is that the events and situations we find most unbearable are actually able to yield:

- Lessons
- Fresh perspectives
- Unexpected gifts
- At the very least, weathering negative emotions teaches us that we can, in fact, survive them!

So, a part of "emotional kung fu" is not to treat negative emotions as an enemy at all, but as a cherished teacher.

Processing Shame Can Help You Develop Compassion

Shame is the painful and humiliating feeling that we are, at our core, wrong somehow.

That we're deficient.

According to expert shame author Brene Brown, "Shame cannot survive being spoken... It cannot survive empathy."

Though the temptation may be to ignore your vulnerabilities and conceal your feelings of inadequacy, Brown claims that this will in fact cut you off from authentic connection with others—which ironically only makes you feel more alone and deficient.

- Acknowledge and own up to feelings of shame.
- Then consciously choose to share those feelings honestly.
→ You may discover a new opportunity to trust others and open up to them.

Hidden gift: genuineness, self-compassion, and connection (and perhaps a little humor).

Processing Cynicism Can Make You More Efficient

If you're not an optimist, use that to your advantage.

If you're always imagining the worst-case scenario, channel that feeling into something useful like

- Planning ahead
- Being prepared
- Doing more than the competition to make sure you come out on top

Pessimism, when guided into action, becomes *shrewdness*, *mental toughness*, and *clarity of vision*.

If you find yourself thinking, "This plan is going to blow up in my face," well, use that. What possible outcomes are your pessimism allowing you to see? Prepare for those.

Hidden gift: productivity.

Processing Envy Can Make You More Congruent With Your Values

Envy *is* an ugly emotion, and one many of us are trained to deny having. But if there is someone you're envious of, embrace that. What does your envy tell you about how you're fulfilling your own potential? What does it imply about the life you'd ultimately want to be living?

Take those feelings of lack and shame and ask what they are saying about what you're truly hungry for. It may be time to use your envy to live a life more congruent with your own values and stop allowing excuses to limit you.

Hidden gift: motivation and self-honesty.

Processing Loss Can Make You More Grateful

Losing something we love is always painful. But even with the most gut-wrenching losses, we can find a gem—the renewed ability to relish what we *do* have.

Loss can be a potent catalyst—if we take control of it and let it steer us somewhere better, that is. Death can be one of the most life-affirming experiences any human can have, and losing everything has a way of reminding you of what's really important.

It can take time to find the blessing in loss, but if you are brave and embrace the sadness, it's an opportunity to go deeper, to find meaning, and to teach yourself new ways of being.

Hidden gift: hope.

Processing Negative Self-Talk Can Make You More Mindful

Negative self-talk can feel like it's with you all the time.

Great!

That means that paying attention to it offers up a chance to connect continuously with the moment. The voice of your inner critic or Saboteur can be like a meditation bell—when you're aware of it, imagine it's like a signal alerting you to something: *"Here's a chance to do something different!"*

As often as you have negative thoughts, you have a new opportunity to change the narrative. In this way, you use your actual experience to bootleg into something better.

If you notice a relentless voice of criticism that follows you around, then rechristen it as the gift of hearing that voice and accepting *it* with compassion every time you notice it.

➔ For example, every time you think, "I'm such a loser for being so negative all the time," let a light bulb go off and tell yourself, "I love and accept you just as you are, and nothing that you can feel is wrong."

Hidden gift: presence and the ability to grow.

In your everyday life, try to keep your ears pricked for clues that you are repressing or denying negative emotions:

- "I'm sorry for being so down today."
- "What's wrong with me?"
- "You're a mess—pull yourself together!"
- "You're overreacting."

Emotions, both positive and negative, are a part of life. They add depth and dimension, keep us safe, and tell us what we care about. And just as we can "surf" strong urges and temptations, we can also ride out strong negative emotions.

How to Metabolize Negative Emotions

Emotional intelligence (EQ) is not just about how well you understand and communicate with others; it's also about how well you know *yourself.*

The only "bad feelings" are those that are not channeled, acknowledged, and allowed to flow on. Emotions that are not "metabolized" this way are still there, only they show up in distorted ways, or else, "What you don't transform, you transmit"—you pass them on to other people.

Step 1: Accept the pain

Your meditation practice will help you acknowledge and face what is without fleeing or resistance. Remember that it is also resistance to want to quickly rush to a solution or to forcefully put a positive spin on things when that's not really what you feel. You don't have to like or agree with how you feel, but try to tolerate it and see that it is indeed how you feel.

Example: A close friend has lied to you, and you're upset. You set aside some time to meditate and journal, breathing and opening up a space for what you feel to just be what it is.

Step 2: Name the pain

Be curious about exactly what you're thinking and feeling. Try to find a word for it, or if you like, think up a symbol or image that conveys your present state.

Metaphors can also help you come to grips with your emotions so that you face them without judgment and shame, but rather curiosity.

Example: After a few minutes, you identify the feeling as anger, but also notice that you're experiencing a strange kind of rejection. You liken it to a car driving by and the passengers flinging their litter out at you—the insult makes your face hot and brings a horrible tight feeling to the back of your throat.

Step 3: Evaluate the pain

Only after you've fully and honestly explored what you feel is it time to start asking what role this emotion is playing in your life right now. Ask what triggered the emotion in the past, what sustains and feeds it in the present, and what potential effects this feeling will have on your behavior and self-concept in the future.

Example: The feeling is close to making you say something hurtful in response. The more you dwell on it, the angrier you seem to feel, but you can see that unchecked, this anger could grow out of proportion.

Step 4: Reconnect to your values and goals

Before you can decide how you're going to harness your emotions and to what end, you need to remind yourself of your overall purpose and any specific goals that take priority.

While you're doing this, try also to remember your strengths and positive attributes, as well as the resources at your disposal. This will broaden the narrowness of perspective that sometimes sets in with a strong negative emotion and gets you back in touch with the bigger context.

Example: You remind yourself that you are a person who is trying their best to be good, and that you would never lie to your friends. You're on a positive path and trying to create the life you want for yourself... which means that you don't tolerate anyone who disrupts that or disrespects it.

Step 5: Find the gift

Reframe what you're experiencing as a potential gift. Make it a game to see how you can tweak your perception until you see what's useful in your present state. Be creative, and even though it might not feel natural at first, try to see if a feeling of gratitude can reveal hidden dimensions about your current situation.

Example: As uncomfortable as it feels, you realize that your anger is trying to tell you something: Stand up for yourself. If you're honest, it's not the first time this friend has violated boundaries or treated you poorly. You mull on this for a while and then thank the anger— it reminded you of what really matters to you. You're grateful for the process of constantly finding people that respect and value you and letting go of ones who don't.

Step 6: Take action

The magic happens when you deliberately choose to channel your emotion into concrete action. Decide what you'll do and do it. You don't need to make major changes or commit to grand action; just take one definite step in the direction of your goals, according to your values, which acknowledged the gift in the motion you feel.

Example: You take a deep breath and promise yourself not to dwell. For the rest of the day, when the thought pops up, you distract yourself or remind yourself of something good in your life. You decide you will put a little distance between you and this friend. Should they lie again to you, you are crystal clear with exactly how you will react to set up a boundary—not with anger, but with calm assertiveness.

Chapter Takeaways:

- Self-disciplined people know that they can choose how they want to feel. Being self-disciplined is not about having no emotions or dominating the emotions you have, but realizing that your conscious will and rational intention are ultimately in charge.
- To use emotions to your own benefit, you need to 1) be aware and 2) reframe. We have to be aware of and honor our emotions, but we mustn't confuse them with an objective appraisal of reality. Just because you feel an emotion doesn't compel you to express it, and controlling your emotions doesn't mean you're being "fake" or emotionally unhealthy.
- "Emotional kung fu" is about turning all emotions, including the negative ones, to our advantage. Negative emotions area inevitable; they can be useful and put to the service of our goals. When you make meaning of your experience and channel it with action, you are in conscious control.
- "Metabolize" shame into self-compassion, cynicism into efficiency and planning, envy into honest evaluation of how congruent your life is to your values, loss into gratitude, and negative self-

talk into an invitation to deeper self-awareness and presence.

- To process any uncomfortable or painful feeling, be aware and accept your reality, give the emotion a name, evaluate it neutrally, remember your goals and values, reframe the experience to find the hidden gift, and finish by taking inspired action in the right direction.